Return To Sender: Hurdles to Horizons

Girl Godsip Series

Book 3

TRACEY R YOUNG

All rights reserved. No part of this publication may be reproduced, distributed, or transmitted in any form or by any means, including photocopying, recording, or other electronic or mechanical methods, without the prior written permission of the publisher, except in the case of brief quotations embodied in critical reviews and certain other noncommercial uses permitted by copyright law.

Printed in the United States of America

Graced Girlfriends, LLC d/b/a Girl Godsip Publishing
PO Box 12569
Beaumont, TX 77726

Copyright © 2025 Tracey R Young

All rights reserved.

ISBN: 979-8-9855876-3-0

DEDICATION

This book is dedicated to my friends and family who have been with me through the storms of life. To those who have called, sent cards, and sent texts just to let me know you were thinking of me, I am grateful. To those who prayed for me silently when I was too devastated to pray for myself, I am thankful. To my pastor, who called me regularly just to hear my voice, pray for me, guide me in the Lord, and encourage me when times were still and the quiet became noisy, you are forever appreciated.

To those who believed in my strength and wished me well to recover, God bless you. I will forever be grateful for my village. To those who didn't believe in me or wished me ill-will, may God continue to bless you as well because He has not given me a spirit of pity, scorn, anger, or resentment: just love, forgiveness, peace, joy, and humility.

To the Lord, my Savior and Redeemer, I am forever grateful for You showing me that YOU will never leave me nor forsake me. I am humbled to be called YOUR daughter. I am exhilarated that YOU are my sender and receiver. Through this journey, Lord, I am honored to say, "By Your stripes, I am HEALED!"

To every person who has felt the pain of rejection from a family member, from a spouse, from a friend, from a confidant, from a co-worker, from a supervisor, from a church member, from a pastor, from a child, from a parent, from a sibling, from your health, from your finances, from your peace, from your tranquility, from your truth, from a stranger, or from any other entity, this book of healing through rejection is dedicated to you. May your journey to your next horizon be filled with enlightenment, healing, courage, and strength.

FOREWORD

When you've lived long enough, you discover that rejection is not a stranger. It comes in many forms—a closed door, an unanswered call, a strained relationship, or even a church pew that doesn't feel as welcoming as it should. As women, we often carry these wounds quietly, unsure if anyone will truly understand the weight of feeling constantly overlooked.

I know this space very personally. After sixteen years of marriage, I faced the painful reality of its end. I had worked so hard to be what I thought was the perfect wife—supportive, loving, kind, and committed. Turns out, in the end….it wasn't enough. The one person I believed would always be there for me was the one who turned away. That season left me feeling unseen and unwanted.

In those dark moments, I clung to God's Word. Isaiah 41:9–10 became a lifeline: *"You are my servant; I have chosen you and not rejected you. So do not fear, for I am with you…"* Those verses reminded me that while human love can falter, God's love never fails. His acceptance is not conditional, nor is it fragile. His embrace is steady, and His promise is secure.

That truth is at the heart of this remarkable book, *Return to Sender*. Tracey R. Young writes with honesty, tenderness, and wisdom. She does not gloss over pain or pretend rejection doesn't hurt. Instead, she opens her own journey to us, reminding us that our scars are not the end of the story.
Through Scripture and lived experience, she shows us that every "no" from the world is met with a resounding "yes" from God!

As a pastor and as a woman, I recognize the sacred courage it takes to put these truths into words. Tracey's meditations invite us not just to survive rejection, but to be reshaped by it. She demonstrates that it's possible to learn, to heal, and to stand again with dignity and faith. Her words remind us that rejection is often God's redirection, and yes, it may sound cliché, but it's true: it also can be God's protection. The very thing that devastated us in our limited view may, in God's broader view, be what protects us from a future we were never meant to carry. What looks like loss to us can become the ground where resilience and faith take root.

So, I encourage you, precious reader, not to rush through these pages. Whether you find yourself standing at a crossroads or simply reading for the joy of it, there's something here for you. Wherever you find yourself, this book will meet you there. Let each reflection settle in your spirit. Journal your own prayers. Sit with the Scriptures. And most of all, allow God to find you in the pages and in the tender places you may have tried to hide.

My prayer is that as you journey through *Return to Sender*, you will come to know with fresh certainty: you are seen, you are loved, and you are never rejected in Christ.

Lynnette Daughtry
Payne Chapel AME Church (Sarasota, FL)

CONTENTS

Introduction	The Gift You Never Wanted	i
Chapter 1	When the Door Closes Without Warning	1
Chapter 2	When the Return is for Your Rescue	11
Chapter 3	The Alignment Assignment	19
Chapter 4	The Bruises that Remind Us	29
Chapter 5	Shedding the Shame	37
Chapter 6	Undeliverable – Address No Longer Valid	47
Chapter 7	The Climb to Clarity	55
Chapter 8	Rebuilding After Rejection	67
Chapter 9	Rediscovering Your Roots and Reclaiming Your Identity	75
Chapter 10	Dignity in the Departure	85
Chapter 11	Commissioned Through the Cracks	91
Chapter 12	The Final Delivery – Signed Sealed & Healed	97

INTRODUCTION

The Gift You Never Wanted
Key Verse

"He heals the brokenhearted and binds up their wounds." — Psalm 147:3

Opening Prayer
Father, as I embark on this journey of healing, open my heart to Your truth. Help me to release the weight of rejection and to see Your divine purpose in every situation. May Your Word bring clarity and comfort. Let me trust that what was meant to break me will be used to bless me. In Jesus' name, Amen.

No one asks for rejection. It arrives at our doorstep like an unwanted package: heavy, burdensome, and often wrapped in pain. We check the label, wondering if it was mistakenly delivered, only to realize it has our name on it. We weren't expecting it. We certainly didn't want it. But there it is, sitting in front of us, demanding to be acknowledged. Rejection doesn't care about timing. It doesn't wait until you're emotionally prepared. It doesn't consider your strengths or past victories. It simply shows up. A spouse walks away, a friendship ends, a job opportunity disappears, a dream slips through our fingers, and, in that moment, the weight of it all can feel unbearable.

Although we may not see it when it happens, rejection is actually a setup, not a death sentence. Rejection often feels like a punishment, as if something is unfairly being taken from us. But what if rejection leads you to something greater? What if the doors that were closed were to protect us from what we could not see?

Throughout Scripture, we see stories of people who faced rejection. People overlooked, cast aside, and betrayed, only to later walk into their God-ordained destiny. Joseph was rejected by his own brothers, sold into slavery, and wrongfully imprisoned. Yet, he later became second in command in Egypt, saving nations from famine (*Genesis 50:20*). David was overlooked by his own father when Samuel came to anoint a king. Yet, he was the one God had chosen (*1 Samuel 16:7*). Even Jesus Himself was despised and rejected (*Isaiah 53:3*), yet His rejection led to our redemption.

This book is about that journey. The journey of returning rejection, healing from it, and embracing the purpose behind it. It's about shifting our focus from what we lost to what God is leading us toward. It's about exchanging our sorrow for His joy, our insecurity for His confidence, and our pain for His promise.

During the writing of this study, I had the opportunity to watch the 2024 Olympics held in Paris, France. As I honed in on one of my favorite categories, gymnastics. I watched with amazement as the U.S. gymnastics team performed on the beam, uneven bars, vault, and floor exercises. History is made during every Olympic competition as the world's best athletes stand proudly on the podium to accept their respective medals.

My next favorite category, track and field, was equally impressive. There was, however, one race that caught my attention, causing me to think at a deeper level—as I tend to do. The Women's 400-meter hurdles. It was during this race that Team USA's Sydney McLaughlin-Levrone shattered a world record to win the gold medal. As she ran out in front of the others, she admitted she thought to herself, *What is behind you will catch up.*

During her follow-up interview, Sydney discussed the importance of training, relationships, support, and knowing you are not alone. She indicated that she is a Believer and leans on her faith. One news station even called her "uncatchable." This was a remarkable description because she was just that—uncatchable—even though she had to jump over hurdles to win. It took years of preparation, fostering relationships, gaining support, and building knowledge for this remarkable athlete to become uncatchable.

As I reflect, I truly believe what this young lady achieved in the physical world is what we should all strive for in the spiritual world: to be uncatchable, despite the hurdles we will face along life's journey. You may be hindered by life's obstacles, knocked over, and have your stride slowed down; however, if we keep God (The Finish Line) in our sight at all times, knowing the enemy remains on our heels constantly, we may also become uncatchable in the spirit. Pace, timing, and awareness are key to outrunning these barriers.

I can forever rest assured of God's perfect timing. Since the completion of *God's Got it in the Bag* and *Woman Absolute*, He has guided me over monstrous hurdles, allowing me to see new horizons I never considered. I have certainly gained a far deeper perspective on the fact that we are genuinely not in control of much other than our own actions.

Life, love, health, finances, relationships, and more are generally the form by which the enemy attacks us because he is always on our heels. Like a runner, we must run knowing what is behind us and trying to catch us if we slow down. The enemy may reach us. However, if we continually run out front, we will be prepared to recognize, leap, and grow through the process. Thus, becoming uncatchable, not getting caught, and not remaining stagnant. It is during the times of most significant growth and hard lessons we find, upon reflection, that we oftentimes became "catchable" rather than uncatchable.

A great deal has transpired in my life since we last met. A cancer diagnosis, loss, divorce, grief, faith-testing, betrayal, family challenges, renewals, hope, enlightenment, recovery, and more. But through it all, my one constant has been God.

We are often taught that if we share our stories, perspectives, and lessons learned with others, and if they truly listen, we may save that person from headaches, trials, and losses, leading them to victory. It is my fervent prayer that every reader of this book gleans early triumph through each chapter. But more so by gathering together to discuss, grow, and build one another up, yielding uncatchable, victorious sisters.

I want this study to be informative, inspiring, and awakening, so I have structured each chapter with a key Bible verse to meditate on, a guided prayer to help you release pain and embrace healing, study questions to deepen your reflection, and a practical activity to help you move forward. You are not alone on this journey. The Lord is walking with you every step of the way.

Guided Activity: Writing a "Return to Sender" Letter

Take a moment to reflect on the most significant rejection you've ever faced. Maybe it's the loss of a relationship, an opportunity that slipped away, or a deep hurt that still lingers. In your journal (or a separate piece of paper), write a "Return to Sender" letter to the Lord.

 - Begin with "Dear Lord, I return this rejection to You."
 - Describe what happened and how it made you feel.
 - Tell God what lies you started believing about yourself because of this rejection.
 - Ask God to replace those lies with His truth.
 - End by thanking God for what He will do through this situation.

When you're done, say this simple prayer:

Lord, I release this rejection into Your hands. I refuse to carry what was never meant for me. Heal my heart, restore my confidence, and help me trust Your plan. In Jesus' name, Amen.

Study Questions for Reflection

1. Can you recall a time when rejection left you questioning your worth?
2. Have you ever seen a rejection later work out for your good? How did it change your perspective?
3. What lies has rejection tried to implant in your heart?
4. How can shifting your mindset from "rejection" to "redirection" change how you see your past experiences?

Rejection is painful, but it does not define you. What was meant to wound you can actually be the very thing that strengthens you. As we begin this journey together, I encourage you to keep your heart open, be honest with yourself, and trust that the Lord is working in ways you cannot yet see. This is not the end of your story; it is the beginning of your healing.

Closing Prayer

Father, I surrender the weight of rejection into Your hands. I refuse to carry what is not mine any longer. Thank You for turning every closed door into a greater opportunity. Thank You for seeing me, loving me, and guiding me. I trust that my rejection is simply a redirection, and I embrace the journey ahead. In Jesus' name, Amen.

CHAPTER ONE
When the Door Closes Without Warning

Key Verse
"See, I have placed before you an open door that no one can shut."
— Revelation 3:8

Opening Prayer

Lord, when doors close in my life, help me to trust that You are leading me to something better. Give me peace in the waiting and clarity to recognize the doors You have opened. I surrender the pain of rejection to You. Teach me to see beyond what was lost and to focus on what You are doing in my life. In Jesus' name, Amen.

Rejection is an unwelcome visitor. It doesn't come with an invitation. It doesn't give us time to prepare or build emotional armor. It arrives unexpectedly, knocking the wind out of us and leaving us wondering what we did wrong. It does not discriminate; it finds its way into friendships, families, careers, and even our faith journey. It escorts itself right into our front doors, takes a seat on our sofa, and puts its feet up on the ottoman, ready to claim our homes, our peace, our relationships, our stability, and, sometimes, our salvation. We must learn to look that enemy straight in the eye and demand that it depart from us, from all that we love, and from all that we hold dear in our lives. And once it departs, we must slam the door shut and set guards in place to ensure our fortress is secure.

In the early 1970s, I was in elementary school, carefree and full of life. I was part of the Bluebirds, a division of the Campfire Girls. My very best friend, who was in the same group, and I were inseparable. We did everything together: laughing, playing, and spending weekends with each other's families. Our bond felt unbreakable. She was of a different ethnicity, but in my home, we were taught that race didn't define a person's value. My mother instilled in us the idea that God created all people, and we were to love everyone accordingly. To me, she was simply my friend and sister.

During the school year, a new girl arrived in our class. She was outspoken, bold, and, in her own way, a leader. But unlike the kind of leader who inspires, she was the kind who controlled. She had a way of making others follow her, even if it meant rejecting those who didn't fit her mold. And one day, she decided that my best friend could no longer be my friend—and she told her just that. My friend was so determined to be a part of the "accepted" group that she did something I would have never expected. She closed the door on our friendship.

With no warning, my world changed. The girl I shared my secrets with, the one I played with at recess, suddenly wanted nothing to do with me. She ignored me, avoided me, and even returned the little notes and candy I had given her, all because the new girl didn't want her to be my friend anymore. I was devastated. At that age, I couldn't grasp the bigger picture. All I could see was that I was no longer enough. It wasn't just the loss of a friend; it was the birth of a lie that whispered, *"You are not worthy."*

I didn't realize it at the time, but this was more than just the end of a childhood friendship. It was the enemy's first attempt at planting the seed of unworthiness in my heart. Rejection has a way of becoming our identity, if we let it. It tells us:

- You're not good enough.
- You don't belong.
- You'll never be chosen.
- You're unlovable.

If left unchecked, these lies take root, affecting how we see ourselves and how we allow others to treat us. Rejection is not a reflection of our worth. It is often a reflection of someone else's pain, insecurities, or circumstances. This is a concept I didn't understand until recently as an adult. Parents, instill this core principle in your children today so they know and understand how to view rejection tomorrow.

When the enemy sends you messages that you're not worthy, stick your chest out and yell, *"I am a child of and loved by the Most High, which means I'm good enough. I am chosen and I am worthy!"*

Looking back, I now see that not every rejection is a loss. Sometimes, it is the Lord's protection. What if my friend wasn't supposed to walk with me for the long haul? What if that friendship, at that time, wasn't meant to continue? What if the Lord allowed that door to close so that I could learn an important lesson, one that I would carry into adulthood and eventually share with others?

I am happy to say I believe both of us learned what "true" friendship was through this circumstance, as we later spoke when the same girl tried to hurt my former friend and wanted to make amends. I am pleased to say that, almost 50 years later, this woman and I are still friends. However, we will never forget the lessons we learned as young children on the day the new girl arrived.

The Lord tells us in *Isaiah 55:8-9, For my thoughts are not your thoughts, neither are your ways my ways, declares the Lord. As the heavens are higher than the earth, so are my ways higher than your ways and my thoughts than your thoughts.*

Rejection stings in the moment, but the Lord's perspective is eternal. What seems like devastation is often redirection. We may cry over the doors that close, but God is already preparing to open new ones that will lead us to His best.

The truth is that rejection will come again. But when it does, we have a choice:

- Will we let it define us?
- Or will we let the Lord refine us?

Instead of seeing rejection as a sign of our inadequacy, we must start seeing it as a redirection toward something greater. The Lord doesn't waste pain. He doesn't allow rejection without purpose. The doors that close, whether in friendships, relationships, jobs, or opportunities, are not meant to break us. They are intended to shape, grow, and prepare us for what's next.

When the Wrong Door Beckons

Grief from rejection doesn't just make you miss what you lost; it also affects your sense of self. It can cause you to forget what you've survived. It convinces you that the door that hurt you might still be the one that holds your future. It plays tricks on your heart, making the familiar feel like safety and the unknown punishment. But sometimes, that thing you're mourning was never intended to be permanent in the first place.

After rejection, we often reach backward, not forward. We return to what we are accustomed to. The relationship that once wounded us, the job that drained us, the friendship that wasn't reciprocal, or the spaces that stifled our growth. We don't go back because it was good. We go back because it's what we know. But God didn't create us for repeat cycles. He made us for forward motion.

And yet, in our fear and confusion, we keep reaching for false doors—doors that look appealing but are covered in spiritual "Do Not Enter" signs. God shuts them with intention, but we try to pry them open with logic, loyalty, desperation, or pride. I know that pattern intimately because I lived it.

Return to Sender: Hurdles to Horizons
Girl Godsip Series: Book 3

The Door That Wouldn't Reopen

I once worked for a hospital I deeply loved. I poured my heart into that place. Not just as a nurse, but as a systems thinker, a problem solver, and a protector of patient care. I created tools, developed accreditation audit tools, anticipated audits, served on committees, and stayed late to ensure our team was always ready. I believed in our mission and our people. It felt like home.

Even while facing health challenges such as my diagnosis of myasthenia gravis, I remained committed. I fought through my physical limitations to make sure the hospital remained excellent. I thought my dedication was enough to secure my place within the company. But one day, without warning, my supervisor walked in and said,

"Tracey, we're undergoing a reduction in force, and your position has been eliminated."

I was stunned. I asked how many people were being let go. Her response shocked me. *"ONE!"*

I called my husband in disbelief. I had done everything in the right way, or so I thought. And now I was the chosen one to be laid off. No notice, no real explanation. I thought, *Okay, I'm a nurse. I'll just transfer to another department. Surely, someone will see my value.*

I recall the number 203. There were exactly 203 job openings in that hospital the day I was laid off. I applied for nine of those positions. I called people I had worked with and reached out to directors who appreciated me. Our nurse recruiter enthusiastically offered me a new role as Nurse Educator. I was excited when I received an offer letter. I accepted and was told, *"You've got the job!"*

But then—radio silence. Three days later, I received a call notifying me that they had to rescind my offer. I asked why of the person I thought was a friend and was told, *"I have no idea, but I have nothing to do with this. I'm so sorry."*

No explanation. Just a closed door.

Seemingly, my applications never reached the hiring managers. Somewhere behind the scenes, I was being blocked. I even considered legal action because I knew something was not legitimate. My then-husband, who also worked for the same hospital, was upset but requested that I bow out gracefully. I knew he was concerned about the possibility of retaliation; I saw it in his face and heard it in his voice. Out of sheer love for him, I didn't pursue any further actions. I walked away with grace. But inside, I was gutted.

I was angry. I was confused. I kept trying to re-enter the same door because I thought it was where I belonged. I couldn't see that it had already served its purpose. And although the Lord had shut it, I wasn't ready to stop knocking.

The Hallway of Hell

I call that season of my life the "hallway of hell." For three weeks, I felt invisible. Unwanted. I had credentials, experience, and excellence, but I couldn't get one foot back inside the place where I had given so much. It felt like betrayal. But what I didn't know was that the hallway was actually a passageway. I just didn't yet recognize it as progress.

Three weeks later, I received a call from another hospital, located outside my immediate area. They had heard about my work and invited me into a new role in their Quality Department. That job became my restoration ground. I brought all the tools and insight I had previously used and applied them in a new setting that welcomed my contribution.

But not long after that, another door opened; this one even greater. When I notified my employer of my decision to leave for growth opportunities, they didn't slam the door. They congratulated me and were excited for my new opportunity, letting me know their door would always be open. I will forever be grateful for the ability to work, even for a short time, at this facility.

A friend from my original hospital (where my door had been closed) had become the Administrator of a local surgery center. He called me very concerned, saying, *"Tracey, we don't have a Quality Department, and we have an accreditation survey upcoming. I need your help."*

So, I joined his team.

I rewrote policies and incorporated updated processes. Some staff members were highly skeptical and handled me with caution because I was a new face implementing unfamiliar policies they had to carry out. However, with these changes, we passed both our accreditation and state surveys with excellence. I was thrilled and felt accomplished. The center felt as though it was the place where the Lord intended me to land.

A while later, I learned that our corporate office had determined our center was at risk of being shut down. My administrator friend was transferred to a stronger facility, so once again I found myself in a hallway. But this time, something different happened.

A few weeks later, the Regional Vice President called. They had seen my work, and without a formal interview, they appointed me as the new Administrator of the surgery center. It was a role I had dreamed of. I attended a medical high school, worked as a registered nurse, and graduated from law school with the goal to someday serve in a higher healthcare administration role. It was everything I thought I lost. And it didn't come through the same door I was banging on. It was through a new one I couldn't even see at the time.

Eventually, the facility was sold to a surgeon whom I had encouraged to buy into our center months earlier. He purchased it, renamed it, and entrusted me to run it. Under our leadership, the facility expanded from three operating rooms to six, added new services, and became one of the busiest ophthalmology and orthopedic centers in the region. Almost daily, I collaborate with the very hospital that once closed its doors to me. However, I hold no bitterness, only gratitude. Because now I understand. That door needed to shut because this is the ONE God meant for me to walk through.

Trusting in the Hallway

We don't always know why doors close. And sometimes, it doesn't matter. What matters is that we stop banging on what God shut and start listening for the sound of Him unlocking something better. False doors are decorated in loyalty, nostalgia, and emotional residue. But divine doors are often hidden in silence, humility, and obedience.

God doesn't ask us to figure everything out. He asks us to trust Him even when it feels like the hallway of hell. Because what looks like a dead end is sometimes just a waiting room for promotion.

Let me tell you something I learned:

🦋 You don't have to shrink to fit the world's version of yourself that God has already delivered you from.
🦋 You don't have to re-enter a door where you've already healed.
🦋 You don't have to explain why you're no longer forcing your way inside.

The hallway hurts. But the hallway also heals. The hallway leads to God's door, not yours.

Guided Activity: Writing a Letter to Your Younger Self

Think back to your earliest memory of rejection.
- What happened?
- How did it make you feel?
- What did it make you believe about yourself?

Now, write a letter to your younger self.

- Tell that child what you now know about rejection.
- Assure them of their worth.
- Speak God's truth over them.

Study Questions for Reflection

1. What door in your life slammed shut, and how did it make you feel? Take a moment to journal about a time when something ended abruptly: a relationship, job opportunity, or friendship. Be honest about the emotions it stirred within you.
2. Looking back, can you see God's protection from that closed door? Has time revealed a reason for the shutdown that you couldn't see at first? What was God sparing you from?
3. Are you still standing in front of that door emotionally? Even if life has moved on, have your thoughts or heart stayed behind? What would it take for you to mentally and spiritually move forward?
4. How do you usually respond to rejection? Do you try to fight for what you lost? Do you internalize the loss? Or do you turn to God for direction? What would a healthy response look like for you?
5. Have you ever mistaken a familiar door for a faithful one? What made it feel right at the time: comfort, fear, loyalty? How can you now discern between familiar doors and those that are God-ordained?
6. What hallway are you standing in right now? Whether it's a season of waiting, uncertainty, or redirection, what would it look like to trust God in this space? Write a hallway prayer that declares your trust, even if you can't yet see the next door.

Remember, healing doesn't always begin with answers; it often starts with awareness. God isn't just the One who closes doors. He's the One who holds the blueprint for every hallway, every detour, and every divine opening ahead. Let this be your encouragement. You are not lost. You are being led. Take your time. Breathe. Revisit these questions as needed. Because sometimes, clarity comes in layers and God reveals it little by little, just enough for the next step.

Closing Prayer

Father, I surrender every rejection I have faced—past and present—into Your hands. Heal the wounds left by closed doors. Teach me to see rejection as Your redirection. Help me trust that You are guiding me to something greater. I release the pain, the questions, and the self-doubt, and I receive Your love and acceptance. In Jesus' name, Amen.

CHAPTER TWO
When The Return is For Your Rescue

Key Verse

"Come to me, all you who are weary and burdened, and I will give you rest."
— Matthew 11:28

Opening Prayer

Father, I bring my wounds of rejection before You. I no longer want to carry this pain, these questions, or this sense of unworthiness. I surrender it all into Your hands. Exchange my sorrow for Your joy, my doubt for Your truth, and my brokenness for Your healing. Help me to trust that You have something better for me. In Jesus' name, Amen.

The Birth of Return to Sender

I never imagined that rejection would come from the person I trusted most in the world. I was married to the person I believed was my soulmate. He was my best friend, my biggest supporter, the other half of me. He stood by my side when I wrote my first book, cheering me on in everything I did. I stood by him through deaths, disappointments, and illness. I was his biggest cheerleader. I thought we had a love that could withstand anything.

But then, without much warning, my world crumbled. We had been going through a rough patch—as many couples do, but I never expected what happened next. One day, I came home, and just like that, he had packed his bags and left. No long conversations. No second chances. Just gone.

It felt as though someone had dropped the weight of the Empire State Building onto my chest. The pain was unbearable. I couldn't eat. I could barely breathe. I spiraled into a depression so deep that I wasn't even sure I wanted to keep living. The questions tormented me: Why wasn't I enough? What had I done wrong? Why would God allow this to happen?

Later, after unsuccessfully trying to restore my marriage, and as I struggled through the fog of heartbreak, one conversation with my ex-husband kept replaying in my mind. He used to tell me that he knew God had sent me to him. He told me (and others), *"I saw a light on you when I first met you, and I knew God sent you to me."*

He always prefaced the phrase by saying he knew it sounded crazy, but he was very serious, and I believed him. I had built my life around that truth. We endured a lot together, but we did it all knowing that we were blessings to one another. But now, I kept thinking if God sent me to him, why did he send me back? It was a thought I wrestled with. How could someone take a blessing from God and return it?

However, the Lord then shifted my perspective. If he truly gave me back to God, then I was given back and placed in the most loving, safest hands possible. He didn't throw me away like I had initially believed. He returned me to the One who had created me, the One who had loved me from the very beginning. And if God had allowed me to be "returned to sender," then maybe—just maybe—this was a divine redirection, not a rejection. Perhaps I wasn't abandoned. Maybe I was being repositioned for something greater.

One of the most powerful lessons I learned through this process was that I had to choose forgiveness, not just for my ex-husband, but for myself. At first, I carried anger, disappointment, and bitterness. I replayed conversations in my mind, trying to find answers to justify my pain. I wanted closure even though I knew I may never receive it. But holding onto unforgiveness was only hurting me, not my ex. I realized that when I returned my pain to the sender, when I gave my heartbreak back to God, I also had to return my anger, resentment, and desire for justice. True healing couldn't happen until I fully released not only my pain, but also my desire to be unforgiving.

Forgiveness didn't mean excusing his actions. It didn't mean saying that what he did was right. It meant choosing freedom over cynicism and animosity. It meant choosing peace over revenge. And most of all, it meant choosing healing over staying trapped in the past. Jesus commands us to forgive in *Matthew 6:14: For if you forgive other people when they sin against you, your heavenly Father will also forgive you.*

I had to make a choice: hold onto the rejection or give it to God and walk in redemption, healing, and peace. It took all the strength, faith, hope, and courage I could muster, but I chose forgiveness. And in doing so, I redeemed myself in the process.

Conceivably, you've been carrying rejection for too long. Maybe you've been abandoned, betrayed, overlooked, or discarded. Perhaps you've asked the same question I did: *"Why wasn't I enough?"*

But what if instead of looking at rejection as a sign of your inadequacy, you started seeing it as God's redirection? What if this heartbreak is not your ending, but your transformation?

When you place rejection into God's hands, you find:

- Peace-where there was once pain.
- Confidence-where there was once insecurity.
- Hope-where there was once heartbreak.
- Freedom-where there was once unforgiveness.

But first, you have to make the exchange. You have to be willing to release the weight of rejection and the grip of unforgiveness so that God can place something better in your hands.

Guided Activity: Writing a "Release the Rejection" Letter

Take a moment to reflect on a rejection that still weighs on your heart—the one you just can't shake—the one that still hurts you to your core at just a thought of your past.

Write a "Release the Rejection" Letter to the person you feel most responsible for this hurt or rejection.

- Begin with "Dear (insert name)"
- Write what you feel happened in detail.
- Tell that person how you feel now and how you have felt since the rejection.
- Write a statement of forgiveness explaining that you are taking the first step of healing yourself by forgiving them. Tell that person you now release them into God's hands.
- Tear that letter apart and throw it in the nearest wastebasket signifying that you are discarding all ties to the discussed circumstances.
- Take a deep breath of RELEASE!

Once you finish, pray this aloud:
God, I release this rejection and unforgiveness into Your hands. I refuse to carry what was never meant for me. Heal my heart, restore my confidence, and help me trust Your plan. In Jesus' name, Amen.

Returned to Myself

I thought I was being rejected. But the truth is, I was being returned, not to those who hurt me, but to me. I was returned to the woman I'd stopped recognizing long ago. I was returned to the voice I'd silenced. I was returned to the life I had adjusted, squeezed, and contorted until it no longer looked like my own. I had been returned to sender, but the sender wasn't just God—it was me—the woman God created in wholeness before heartbreak, before disappointment, and before sacrifice became silence.

Return to Sender: Hurdles to Horizons
Girl Godsip Series: Book 3

By the time the return slip was attached to my life, my children were grown. My youngest had one semester left in college. My oldest was living on his own. The house was quiet. But it was the kind of quiet that screams. The type of quiet that echoes with absence and unanswered questions. My husband was gone, and with him went my routine: the structure, the rhythm, the normal. But what hit me hardest wasn't the silence; it was the fact that I no longer knew who I was inside of it.

I went to work every day because I was needed. I showed up for my patients, for my responsibilities, and for the things that kept me functioning. But when I came home, I collapsed into the quiet as it reminded me: you're alone. And not just alone in your house. Alone in your soul. I had lost my taste buds. Lost my laugh. Lost my favorite music. Lost the woman who once knew how to make a home and wasn't dependent on another person being there to feel alive in it.

I went into the kitchen one morning, attempting to cook breakfast. Something simple. And I stood there frozen, staring at the stove, asking myself a question I hadn't asked in years: What do I like to eat? I didn't know. For so long, I had cooked what my former spouse liked. Bought what he wanted. Watched what he enjoyed. Adjusted myself to his preferences, even down to the television schedule.

I loved basketball and grew up in a basketball family. I taught my son how to shoot a free throw. But my husband preferred football, and somewhere along the line, I stopped watching basketball altogether. It wasn't a big fight. And it was not something he ever asked of me. It was just a slow, quiet erosion that I didn't even realize was happening.

Even in our rocky season, I kept the routine. I stayed in sync with my spouse because that's what good wives do, right? I believed I was honoring God by showing reverence to my husband. But one day, in my extreme brokenness during a conversation with a close friend, she said something that pierced me:

"Tracey...you made your husband into a little god!"

I immediately disagreed. I'm a Believer. I know there's only one God. I loved my husband, yes, but I never put him before the Lord. Correct? But the more I sat with this thought, the more I saw the truth. I had centered so much of myself around his wants, his ways, his needs, that my identity blurred. I filtered decisions, plans, and even convictions through the lens of his reaction. I thought I was being a godly wife. Still, in some ways, I had sacrificed too much of my own relationship with God to keep peace in my relationship. So when the marriage ended, it devastated me.

Not just because I loved him, but because I had given him a throne he never asked to sit on. I'd elevated him beyond what was fair to him and what was right before God. That wasn't his doing. It was mine. That's why the "return" cut so deep. That's why the pain wasn't just heartbreak. It was identity loss. The pain of the return wasn't just about losing my marriage. It was about realizing I had lost myself.

There's the miracle: God didn't return me because I was broken. He returned me because I was being preserved. He loved me too much to let me continue blending in and disappearing. He loved me too much to let my identity be filtered through someone else's preferences. He knew that for me to live—truly live—I had to be returned to myself.

And this isn't just my story.

Some people lose themselves in marriages. Others lose themselves in jobs, friendships, ministries, or status. We make idols out of people, platforms, and expectations without even realizing it. And when it ends, when it's stripped away, when we're returned to sender, we don't just grieve their loss. We grieve the loss of the self we sacrificed.

As of the writing of this book, I still haven't started dating. I was faithful in my marriage and dedicated to one man. I'm not sure what being with someone else looks like for me, and I most certainly will not rush into anything God didn't ordain. After the divorce, I spoke to my ex-husband about the possibility of future reconciliation. His answer quickly reminded me that God had closed this door. And this time, I didn't run to reopen it.

Instead, I've focused on repairing the one relationship that truly matters: my relationship with God. My real God. Not the little gods I created in the name of love or loyalty. Not the ones I served out of fear of being alone. But the One who never asked me to shrink to be loved. The One who never left me in the silence. The One who returned me to me. And I'm learning that being alone with God isn't loneliness. It's healing. It's clarity. It's peace.

Whether God sends someone new into my life or not, I'm committed to this truth: No one else will ever sit on the throne God alone deserves.

I am whole.
I am loved.

And I've been returned to the woman I was always meant to be.

Answer these questions as you quietly reflect on this moment:

- Have you ever lost yourself in someone or something else?
- Are there pieces of you that you've silenced to keep peace or to avoid conflict?
- Who or what have you made into a "little god", even unintentionally?

God is not in the business of rejection. He's in the business of redirection. Sometimes, in His mercy, He lets it all fall apart so that you can fall back together in Him. Now isn't this a beautiful thing? I pray this changes your perspective on being returned to sender.

Study Questions for Reflection

1. What rejection are you still carrying that needs to be returned to God?
2. How has rejection shaped the way you see yourself?
3. How does knowing that Jesus experienced rejection help you in your healing process?
4. What do you think God is trying to exchange your rejection for: peace, confidence, joy?
5. Who do you need to forgive in order to fully release rejection?
6. Have you ever adjusted your identity, preferences, or voice to keep someone else comfortable? What did it cost you?
7. In what ways have you unintentionally made someone or something into a "little god" in your life? What might God be asking you to release?
8. What is one practice or passion you used to enjoy that you want to reconnect with as you return to the woman God created you to be?

Sometimes God allows the return not to punish you, but to preserve you. In the unraveling, He reveals the pieces of yourself that were buried beneath obligation, silence, or survival. This chapter invites you to see rejection not as a loss, but as a holy redirection. You are not just being returned—you are being restored. And this time, you are returning to the One God always intended you to be.

Closing Prayer

God, thank You for returning me, not just from broken places, but to sacred spaces within myself that I had forgotten. Forgive me for placing people, routines, or roles above You. Thank You for showing me that what I thought was rejection was actually Your protection. Restore the parts of me that got buried under people-pleasing and survival. Bring clarity where there was confusion, and peace where there was pain. Help me never again give someone the seat that only You deserve.
May I always know who I am because I'm anchored in who You are.
In Jesus' name, Amen.

CHAPTER THREE
The Alignment Assignment

Key Verse

"Do not conform to the pattern of this world, but be transformed by the renewing of your mind. Then you will be able to test and approve what God's will is—His good, pleasing and perfect will." —Romans 12:2

Opening Prayer

Father God, thank You for designing me with purpose and intention. Help me to release the need for outside approval and instead anchor my worth in You. Teach me to realign my life with Your divine blueprint. Where I have been swayed by rejection, please heal me. Where I have been discouraged, reignite the fire of purpose. Let this chapter be a holy recalibration; one that reminds me who I am and whose I am. In Jesus' name, Amen.

The Fire Within: Perfectly Aligned

Rejection, left unaddressed, can cause severe misalignment in our lives. From our earliest moments, we are hardwired with a longing to be seen, known, and accepted. As children, we quickly learned that smiles and good behavior earn praise and approval through stickers, applause, and rewards. This is a lesson we carry into adulthood.

I remember vividly how my mother created a special star chart for me. It was her loving way of encouraging responsibility and reward, wrapped in creativity and care. This chart wasn't a formal contract or a rigid system. It was a colorful piece of poster board that hung proudly in our home. She used a ruler to draw straight lines across and down, forming a grid. On the left-hand side were tasks, everyday things I was expected to do: Make your bed before school, Empty the trash cans, Put away the dishes, Finish your homework, Say your prayers before bed, etc. They were simple chores, woven into our daily rhythm.

But that chart transformed the ordinary into something extraordinary. Each time I completed a task, I placed a shiny sticker in the corresponding square. I can still remember the feeling of peeling off a new sticker and carefully pressing it onto the chart, as if I were adding a medal to a trophy case. However, it wasn't just about the sticker; it was about what the sticker meant. I was doing a good job. It meant I was seen. It meant I was celebrated. And when I earned enough stickers, a prize was waiting at the end. Sometimes it was a small toy or an extra hour of television, which was a big deal back then since we didn't have on-demand cartoons or streaming channels. Television time was precious and limited.

Occasionally, the prize was getting to stay up past my bedtime to watch a special movie on one of those old video discs encased in clunky plastic casings that we slid into a bulky machine. That was the reward. That was alignment. I did the right thing, and I received a reward. I met the expectation, and I was accepted.

But even as I grew older, that system stayed with me. I may have outgrown the star chart, but I didn't outgrow the need for affirmation. I found myself chasing stars; only now they were grades, promotions, social approval, relationships, likes, and praise. I still measured my worth by how many "stickers" I earned in someone else's eyes.

And so many of us do the same. We keep invisible charts in our minds, tallying approval and affirmation from every direction. We overextend ourselves trying to check off what we think will finally earn us a sense of belonging. But something shifts when we realize that we've spent so much time trying to fit into a chart that we've forgotten how to fit into our calling.

That's where the lesson of alignment comes in.

As children, shows like *Sesame Street* and *Mr. Rogers' Neighborhood* taught us more than letters and numbers. They shaped how we saw ourselves. *Sesame Street* gave us knowledge. *Mr. Rogers' Neighborhood* gave us a sense of identity. Each time Mr. Rogers exited the screen with his gentle voice and warm eyes, changing out of his cardigan and sneakers, he reminded us in his song *It's Such A Good Feeling* that, *"You always make each day such a special day. You know how? By just you're being you!"* His intent was for every child to feel valued, secure in their own skin and special at the end of every episode—to say to each child, "You are enough!"

Mr. Rogers taught us about feelings. About kindness. About belonging. He sang songs such as:

"It's you I like.
It's not the things you wear,
It's not the way you do your hair
But it's you I like.
The way you are right now,
The way down deep inside you…"

But even with all that truth, we still got caught up in performance.

Because life taught us something else: approval is conditional. Belonging is earned. Rejection hurts. We learned early that acceptance can be given, and it can be taken away. And so we molded ourselves accordingly. We shaped our personalities to avoid pain, to earn applause, to remain accepted. We began to believe that being ourselves wasn't enough. And if it's not, why are we even doing it?

And this is where the misalignment begins. When we adjust ourselves so much to fit the world, we often edge out the very purpose God placed within us. You can feel it in your spirit when you're out of alignment. It feels like an uneasiness. Like carrying joy with a limp. Like you're doing everything "right," but you still feel wrong inside. You smile for the photos, show up for the meetings, get the praise, and still go home feeling unfulfilled.

Why? Because purpose isn't about performance. It's about positioning.

There is a fire inside of you; a divine flame lit by God Himself. But here's the truth: that fire can only burn when you are aligned.

I remember playing with magnifying glasses as a kid. We'd go outside on sunny days, take a magnifying glass, and look for a dry patch of grass or leaves. Then we'd slowly adjust the angle of the glass until the sunlight focused into a tiny, burning beam. And if everything aligned just right—the sun, the glass, and the target— a fire would ignite. Not because we forced it. Not because we begged for it. But because we had everything in order. That's the power of alignment.

The sun was always shining. The magnifying glass was always present. The ground was always dry. But the fire didn't come until everything was in the proper position. Purpose works the same way. The fire in your soul—the calling, the clarity, the power—won't ignite through hustle alone. It ignites when you come into alignment with God's will.

That fire is your confirmation. It's your signal. It's your spiritual yes.

And when you begin to live in alignment, you stop needing sticker charts and external applause.
You no longer live for someone else's idea of success. You live for God's direction. You trade striving for stillness. You exchange applause for the assignment.

Alignment teaches:
You are not loved because of what you do.
You are not valuable because you produce.
You are not accepted because you meet expectations.
You are loved because God created you.
You are valuable because He formed you.
You are accepted because Jesus paid the price for you.

And when that truth gets deep into your spirit, no rejection can uproot it. You begin to walk differently. You begin to trust differently. You're not working for a reward; you're walking in relationship. You're not begging for fire; you're living in alignment. And that is where transformation begins.

Rejection Broke My Heart, But God Realigned My Soul

There's a deep kind of pain that comes from being told, directly or indirectly, that you're not enough. Maybe it was a parent who withheld love. A friend who ghosted you without explanation. A job that chose someone else. A partner who picked another path. A church that celebrated your gifts but ignored your grief. Rejection doesn't always announce itself. It often presents itself in the form of silence, withdrawal, or a closed door.

What makes rejection so hard is not just the event itself; it's what it awakens in us. We start asking dangerous questions: What did I do wrong? What's wrong with me? Why wasn't I chosen? We begin to equate the absence of acceptance with the lack of worth.

That's how rejection becomes more than a moment. It becomes a mindset. And mindsets become prisons.

You start living in reaction mode—overthinking every word, replaying old conversations, second-guessing your instincts. You shrink. You settle. You silence your voice for the sake of being palatable to others. But God never called you to be palatable. He called you to be powerful.

Here's the sacred truth: Rejection didn't ruin you. It revealed what was misaligned.

Some relationships didn't end because you were flawed. They ended because your growth no longer fit the other person's comfort zone. Some platforms didn't open because your voice was too small, but because your message was too bold. You were never rejected because you weren't worthy. You were redirected because you were evolving.

And that evolution required realignment.

Realignment is God's way of adjusting the lens through which you see yourself. It's not about fixing your flaws. It's about re-centering your faith.

When you live in alignment, your decisions shift. You stop begging for a seat at tables that weren't built with you in mind. You stop explaining your no. You stop apologizing for the light God has placed inside you.

You realize: You were not rejected. You were rerouted.

God's rerouting doesn't come with neon signs or easy answers. Sometimes it looks like isolation. Sometimes it feels like heartbreak. But what it always leads to is clarity. You gain clarity on your calling, clarity on your worth, clarity on your identity. You begin to see yourself the way heaven sees you, not as a sum of your wounds, but as a vessel still worthy of being used.

You're no longer interested in flawless presentation. You're interested in peace. You stop trying to impress and start trying to obey. You're not performing; you're positioning. You stop striving for someone's approval and start standing in God's assignment. You stop needing constant affirmation from others and start walking in daily affirmation from the Holy Spirit. You remember who you were before rejection made you forget.

And that remembering is a holy revolution.

Rejection broke your heart, yes. But it also broke the false narratives that had no business being there in the first place. It shattered the illusions of needing to earn love, prove value, or validate your identity.

And in the wreckage, God rebuilt you. Stronger. Clearer. Aligned. Now, your yes means more because it's not coming from desperation. It's coming from discernment. You're not just walking through life hoping to be seen. You're walking through life knowing you were meant to be. Alignment doesn't make life perfect. It makes your path purposeful.

When rejection tries to tell you again, "You're not enough," you'll smile, not in arrogance, but in awareness. You'll say, *"That may be true for others, but I'm more than enough for the One who sent me."*

Because now, you're not asking, *"Why didn't they choose me?"* You're thanking God for the realignment.

Guided Activity: The Realignment Reset

Purpose: To help you recognize areas of misalignment in your life and invite God into the process of spiritual, emotional, and purpose-based realignment.

Step 1: Inventory Your Alignment
1. Where do I feel the most tension or unrest in my life right now?
2. Am I making decisions based on fear of rejection or alignment with God's will?
3. What have I been clinging to that no longer fits the version of me God is shaping?

Step 2: Your Realignment Declaration
God, I give You full access to every part of my life.
If it's misaligned, correct it. If it's out of place, reposition it.
If it's rooted in fear, replace it with faith.
I release the weight of rejection and receive the strength of realignment.
I declare that I will no longer live for the approval of others,
but for the purpose You've placed in me.
I am not lost—I am being aligned.
In Jesus' name, Amen.

Step 3: Create a "Non-Negotiables" List
Write down three non-negotiables you will honor from this day forward to stay aligned:
- I will not _____
- I will no longer accept _____
- I will prioritize _____

Return to Sender: Hurdles to Horizons
Girl Godsip Series: Book 3

Study Questions for Reflection

1. What were some early messages you received about acceptance and approval growing up?
2. In what ways has rejection shaped your identity or behavior?
3. How do you define alignment in your current season of life?
4. Can you recall a specific rejection that turned out to be a redirection toward something better?
5. How do you recognize when you're out of alignment with God's purpose?
6. What internal lies have you believed because of past rejection?
7. What new truths can you replace those lies with, based on Scripture?
8. What does it look like for you to live in spiritual alignment every day?
9. What habits or people support your alignment? Which ones sabotage it?
10. How does accepting that God sent you change the way you view rejection?

Closing Prayer

Heavenly Father, thank You for being the anchor when rejection tried to shake me. Thank You for the divine hand that realigns what life tries to scatter. I no longer want to live for approval, applause, or appearance. I want to live in alignment with truth, with peace, with You. Heal every place in me that was wounded by rejection. Fill the gaps where insecurity tried to take root. Replace every fear with faith. Teach me to walk boldly in my assignment, even when the crowd doesn't understand, even when the door closes, even when the invitation doesn't come. Because I now know that I wasn't rejected. I was redirected. And I say yes to alignment, to purpose, and to becoming who You created me to be. In Jesus' name, Amen.

CHAPTER FOUR
The Bruises That Remind Us

Key Verse

"No weapon that is formed against you shall prosper, and every tongue that shall rise against you in judgment you shall condemn. This is the heritage of the servants of the Lord, and their righteousness is from me," says the Lord.
— Isaiah 54:17

Opening Prayer

Heavenly Father, I come before You today, tender and open. There are bruises in my life—visible and invisible—that ache as reminders of pain and rejection. But I know You are the Healer, the Comforter, and the One who lifts me out of despair. As I walk through this chapter, I open my heart to Your truth. Show me how even the bruises can become testimonies of healing, restoration, and Your perfect love. In Jesus' name, Amen.

The Bruise Was The Blessing

Bruises leave marks that fade and eventually go away. But they hurt, sometimes deeply and for longer than we expect. Some leave noticeable discolorations that become daily reminders of moments we'd rather forget. The thing about bruises is that they represent impact, that something hit us, something jarred us, something wounded us, even if it didn't break us.

I remember all too well falling in my driveway just a few months ago. It was raining, and I was alone. I slid on the pebble driveway and tore right through my new jeans. When I looked down, my knee was busted open, bleeding everywhere. I must have tried to break my fall because my hand was also cut, bruised, and throbbing.

My first instinct? Jump up and look around. Did anybody see me fall? I wasn't even worried about the blood. I was more concerned about embarrassment. Isn't that just how rejection works?

Rejection wounds us, yes. But it also embarrasses us, especially when it's public. Whether it's a marriage that ended, a friendship that crumbled, or a job we didn't get, there's always this instinct to cover it up, to pretend it didn't happen. But sisters, we did fall. And that's okay.

I limped into the house, swapped out my jeans, and cleaned my cuts. I then realized that several glass shards were sticking out of my knee. I attempted to remove them but was very worried that I had missed some and knew this could mean trouble later. Out of an abundance of caution, I headed to the local emergency clinic for X-rays of my knee and hand, and to ensure all traces of glass were removed.

My knee was throbbing. My hand was burning, and I could barely move my small finger. I remember thinking that something must be broken. It has to be. The swelling, the pain, the stiffness convinced me of this. But after the X-rays and evaluation, the nurse practitioner told me:

"Nothing is broken. You're just banged up pretty bad. But tomorrow...tomorrow will feel worse. You'll feel like someone beat you up. But after that, the healing begins."

Those words stuck with me: *"Tomorrow will feel worse."*

Isn't that the truth about rejection?

Today stings.
But tomorrow...it'll hurt.
Tomorrow is when it sinks in.
Tomorrow is when you cry.
Tomorrow is when you feel it deep in your bones and your spirit.
But the beautiful thing? Healing comes after tomorrow.

The nurse warned me about the bruises, the aches, the stiffness. And she was correct. But she also promised healing. And she was right about that as well.

Just like physical bruises, emotional bruises don't mean we are broken. Even if we are, God is a Master Healer. He created our physical bodies with the ability to heal wounds over time. Because God cares so much, how much more will He tend to our hearts?

Let's dive deeper. Rejection will try to convince you that you're broken beyond repair. But that's a lie. Rejection will try to define you. But it doesn't. Rejection will bruise you. But you will heal.

Here's what I learned through that fall and many others before it. The fall doesn't define me. The getting up does.

I realized I had been treating emotional rejection the same way I treated that fall.
- Jumping up fast.
- Pretending it didn't hurt.
- Hiding the bleeding.
- Hoping no one saw.

But healing doesn't happen in hiding. Healing requires acknowledging the bruise, treating the wound, and giving yourself permission to rest and recover. The bruise is not the end. You may hurt today. You may hurt tomorrow. But you won't hurt forever. That's a promise.

The swelling will go down. The pain will ease. The scar may remain, but even that will fade. And it will become a testimony, not a reminder of trauma. You're not broken. You're becoming the healing oil for your wounds.

There's something sacred about oil. Something healing. Something divine.

In Scripture, oil was never just a household remedy. It was a spiritual signpost. Kings were anointed with it. Priests were consecrated by it. The sick were healed through it. Oil represented covering, covenant, healing, authority, and the tangible presence of God. It wasn't random that the Good Samaritan in *Luke 10* didn't just bandage the wounded traveler; he poured in the oil and the wine. Oil soothed what was broken. It softened the bruises. It signaled care and restoration.

I didn't fully grasp the magnitude of that symbolism until I found myself bruised, not just physically but also emotionally. Not just scraped knees, but a scraped soul. I was deep in a season of depression that I revealed to almost no one except my pastor and closest friends, most of whom I even kept at a distance. My body showed up, but my spirit felt absent.

During this time, I was enrolled in an Integrative Aromatherapy Nursing Certification Program, where I learned about the holistic healing properties of essential oils. How lavender can calm the mind; how frankincense can ease anxiety; how peppermint can bring clarity. I was studying the same oils God designed in His wisdom through the plants of the earth. However, I chose to set my lessons aside to wallow in my sadness. When my emotional pain took over, I shelved the healing tools that surrounded me. The oils. The books. The faith. I didn't reach for them. I sat in misery even though healing was nearby.

It wasn't until I had fallen, as described earlier—this time, physically—that things began to shift. You see, I've always prided myself on not having many scars on my legs, despite being a tomboy at heart. I climbed trees, jumped fences, and played hard. Yet somehow, the bruises faded, the scratches healed, and the scars never stayed. This was a blessing as I reached my high school and young adult years, when wearing dresses, skirts, and shorts took the place of jeans. After all, who wanted to look at scarred legs on a girl?

I remember visiting my grandmother, whose home was where I generally received the cuts and bruises. I played outside with the neighborhood kids, unlike at my home, where most of my activities were indoors. Oftentimes at my grandmother's house, I'd come inside crying from another outdoor mishap. She'd reach into her medicine cabinet and pull out a small green bottle of Campho-Phenique, a mysterious, oily substance I knew nothing about. She'd rub it gently onto my skin, place a bandage over the cut, and send me back out to play. Sometimes, if I felt a bit spoiled, I'd stay inside and trade in my tomboy feats for girly activities with her. If it still hurt, she'd apply more oil. Although I didn't know what was in the oil, I knew that it worked. It healed my wounds, and the scars disappeared.

On another occasion, about 30 years later, I fell into an uncovered pool filter opening in my brother's backyard when the contractors mistakenly forgot to cover it after installation. It was then, in my late 40s, that I received my first lasting scar. I still believe I wouldn't have this scar if I had not received stitches. And just a few months ago, at 54, I had a repeat. Yes, the driveway fall was next, complete with broken skin, embedded glass shards, and, eventually, a visible scar.

My desire to avoid a permanent physical scar drove me to act. I picked up everything God had already equipped me with—knowledge, training, insight—and began mixing oils with intention. My healing hands, guided by the Spirit, anointed my wound with faith. And suddenly, *Psalm 23:5* came alive: *"You anoint my head with oil; my cup overflows."*

But then it hit me: Why hadn't I treated my emotional scar with the same intentionality and urgency?

I had anticipated the physical scar, so I launched into immediate action to minimize its permanence. But when the emotional wounds came—abandonment, disappointment, depression—I didn't apply spiritual oil. I didn't reach for the oil of the Lord. I didn't anoint my mind with the promises of God.

Isaiah 61:1 says, *"The Spirit of the Lord…has anointed me to bind up the brokenhearted."* And yet, I let my heart bleed. I didn't pick up my tools. I didn't fight for my healing until the scar on my knee reminded me. That driveway fall wasn't just about broken skin. It was God's wake-up call: *"I've already given you the oil. Use it."* Just like the Good Samaritan, I had to pour oil and wine into myself.

The Lord showed me that my bruises weren't formed to break me. They were designed to bless someone else through me. Even bruises need oil. So I returned to my course. I picked up my books, flipped through my essential oil guides, and reviewed how frankincense soothes emotional trauma. I began to recognize that *James 5:14* wasn't only about sickness of the body; it was about anointing the weary soul as well.

I called my instructor and admitted that I had been knocked down by life but told her I was ready to complete my certification. I worked diligently and with purpose. I finished my studies, earning the title of Certified Integrative Aromatherapy Nurse. But more importantly, I rediscovered my anointing.

At this time, I picked up my pen to finish writing *Return To Sender: From Hurdles to Horizons*. I poured oil into my own emotional wounds, page by page. With every chapter, God restored me. *Ecclesiastes 9:8* says, *"Let your garments always be white, and let oil not be lacking on your head."* I realized the oil was never lacking. I had just stopped applying it.

When I finally did, healing flowed. Purpose returned. And now, I carry both the oil and the testimony. Because what the enemy thought would leave me scarred for life, God anointed to bring healing to others.

Return to Sender: Hurdles to Horizons
Girl Godsip Series: Book 3

Guided Activity: Journaling

Journal Prompt 1:

Recall a time when you felt emotionally bruised—not shattered, but sore in the soul.
- Who or what caused the bruise?
- How did you react?
- What (or who) did you turn to or not turn to?

Journal Prompt 2:

Reflect on whether you reached for "oil"—a soothing balm of Scripture, prayer, worship, rest, or community.
- Did you allow yourself to heal?
- What tools were within reach that you may have ignored at the time?

Journal Prompt 3:

How might you respond differently next time? What spiritual oils do you now recognize are already within reach?

Affirmation to Speak Aloud:

"Even when life leaves me bruised, I will not ignore the oil. I am worthy of healing. I am anointed for restoration. And God is not finished with me yet."

Study Questions for Reflection

1. Can you recall a time when emotional pain felt just like physical pain?
2. Why do you think we're so quick to hide our pain from others?
3. What does the phrase "healing begins after tomorrow" mean to you personally?
4. In what ways do you see God tending to your emotional bruises even now?
5. How does *Psalm 147:3* encourage you in your current season?
6. What "oil" has God already placed in your life that you may have overlooked, such as spiritual gifts, relationships, healing practices, or wisdom?
7. Can you recall a time when you focused on physical or external healing while ignoring emotional or spiritual wounds? What did that reveal about your patterns of care?
8. The Good Samaritan poured in both oil and wine, then promised to return. How does this image of continual, compassionate care reshape your view of God's presence in your healing?
9. When you consider your current season of life, is there a place within you in need of oil? What would it look like to anoint that space with prayer, rest, Scripture, or truth?

Closing Prayer

Lord, thank You for seeing every bruise — even the ones I hide from the world. Thank You for being a God who doesn't just notice my pain but promises to heal it. I ask You to come into the broken places, the bruised places, and the deeply wounded areas of my life. Teach me not to hide my pain but to place it gently in Your hands. May I walk boldly in the truth that I am not broken beyond repair. I am being restored. In Jesus' name, Amen.

CHAPTER FIVE
Shedding the Shame

Key Verse:

"Those who look to Him are radiant; their faces are never covered with shame."
—Psalm 34:5

Opening Prayer:

Father, I come before You, laying down every burden of shame, every whispered lie of the enemy, and every heavy garment that You never meant for me to wear. Wrap me in Your truth. Remind me of who I am in You. Restore to me the joy of Your salvation, and clothe me with righteousness, not regret. In Jesus' name, Amen.

When Shame Speaks Louder Than Truth

There is a quiet yet heavy weight that accompanies rejection: shame. It's not loud like anger or sharp like grief. It's subtle, slippery, and suffocating. It creeps in when you least expect it and murmurs, *"It's your fault."*

Shame convinces us that our rejection is deserved and that our brokenness disqualifies us from healing. It doesn't just speak in words; it settles in the bones, in the shoulders, and in the spirit.

In 2022, just a year before the dissolution of my marriage, I received a diagnosis that no one wants to hear: stage four neuroendocrine cancer. The doctors were kind, compassionate, and blunt. They told me it was not curable, but treatable. They explained that it was something I would live with for the rest of my life. I heard them, but I did not place my trust in their words. I put my trust in God. Because while medicine may have limitations, my God does not. Their diagnosis was factual, but it wasn't final.

I've seen God heal. I've experienced it before. Years ago, I was diagnosed with myasthenia gravis. Through prayer and a complete shift to holistic methods, I saw restoration in my health. I stepped away from many of the medications, leaned heavily into God's word, and saw my body respond in miraculous ways. So when I faced this new diagnosis, I was instantly reminded that healing is not new to my God. I had walked with Him through valleys before, and this time would be no different.

In hindsight, I realized that during that time, I had leaned more on my husband than on God. And when he walked away, I realized I had forgotten who my real anchor was. God had to gently but firmly remind me: *"Lean on Me."* And that lesson, though painful, was pivotal.

In my journey of integrative aromatherapy and holistic healing, I sought out a practitioner who specialized in these areas of medicine, not just for treatment, but also for alignment. He prayed with me. He laid hands and rebuked cancer in Jesus' name. And then he asked a question that lingered like incense in the air: *"Are you carrying shame?"*

At first, I said no. But the question haunted me. I sat with it. Prayed over it. Reflected on it. And slowly, the bricks began to surface. The shame I thought I had buried began to rise.

I was ashamed that I got pregnant before marriage, even though we married, but eventually divorced. I was ashamed it took me ten years to get my degree because I'd married so young. I was ashamed I had survived domestic violence but never told a soul. I was ashamed of being married more than once. I was ashamed that despite being faithful, grounded, and God-loving, my husband packed a bag and walked away. We worked in the same community, so I was ashamed because our separation was public. We were seen as a power couple. And now, I was a woman walking around with a broken heart and a silent scream.

People whispered. I heard lies. I confronted rumors that were denied, but I knew they were true. And worst of all, I was caught in a cycle of trying to explain, trying to prove, trying to maintain my image while privately drowning in embarrassment.

And then there was the cancer. I'm not saying my marital break caused the cancer because it was there approximately nine months before my ex-husband's exit. But, according to the holistic practitioner, the shame that came with it certainly didn't help and could have been blocking my holistic healing. This was my burden to bear. Everything—all of it—was an emotional and spiritual weight I was already carrying. It was like a layered garment: first rejection, then shame, then silence until I could no longer breathe under the strain of it all.

Through prayer, study, and deep reflection, I learned that rejection is often the gateway to shame. And shame, when not dealt with, creates a cycle:

Rejection → Shame → Silence → Bitterness → Broken Identity

That cycle is deadly. Not just spiritually, but physically. Shame and guilt don't just torment the mind; they can manifest in the body. The holistic doctor told me that gastrointestinal cancers, among others, are often rooted in emotional distress, especially shame. And in my quiet moments, I believed him. The body keeps the score. What the heart suppresses, the body expresses.

I began to see the enemy's strategy: to trap me in shame so that I would stop speaking, stop healing, and stop believing. The shame silenced me. It isolated me. It made me forget who I was and whose I was. But God.

God began to show me a new cycle:

Rejection → Release → Healing → Redemption → Restoration

God reminded me of *Matthew 11:28*: *"Come to Me, all you who are weary and burdened, and I will give you rest."*

Shame is a burden. And Christ is our rest.

I started waking up every day with a new declaration: *"I'm not who they say I am. I'm not my past. I'm not my mistakes. I'm not my timeline. I'm not my divorce. I'm not my diagnosis. I am a daughter of the Most High."*

I began to shed shame like old skin. It didn't happen overnight. Some mornings I still felt its chill. But I learned to rebuke it. I learned to speak to it. I learned to recognize it for what it was: a lie.

You see, shame isn't just about what happened to you. It's about what you believe it says about you. But Jesus died so that you would be free from that lie. You are not what you've been through. You are not what they whispered. You are not your broken moment.

Shame has no place in your calling.

If you're reading this, and your heart is heavy with shame over your past, your relationships, your health, or your choices, hear this: God is not ashamed of you. He's not embarrassed by you. He loves you. He redeems you. And He is not finished with you.

Let Him rewrite your narrative.

You no longer have to wear shame as a name tag. God has called you by name, not by mistake. He sees you through the lens of grace, not gossip. Through the eyes of mercy, not memory. Through the filter of His promise, not your past.

You are not the one who failed. You are the one who endured!

Break the cycle. Shed the shame. Step into restoration. Let the shame fall to the floor like the grave clothes that once bound Lazarus. Come forth, daughter. Rise in truth. Walk in grace.

From Shame to Shine – Becoming Radiant Again

There comes a moment when you have to say, *"Enough."*

Enough of letting shame write the story. Enough of hiding. Enough of rehearsing regrets and crawling through the past. One day, I looked in the mirror and realized I had allowed shame to silence me, steal my joy, and dim my light. And I decided, I was done!

Shame had walked beside me long enough. It had silently told me that I wasn't enough. That just because of divorce, diagnoses, or disappointment, I no longer had value. However, the truth was that I was never alone in my suffering, and I was never without purpose. I had to realize that I was not broken beyond repair. I was simply in the process of becoming. I had been reshaped. Yes. Pressed and bruised. Yes. But never disqualified.

What changed? When I started looking around, I noticed that everyone has something in common. Everyone has a story, a heartbreak, a bruise, and a past. We all walk through hallways of hardship. And with that realization, I found freedom. I wasn't the exception. I was simply human. My pain was not proof of failure. It was evidence of living.

That truth set me free!

I stood in front of the mirror and spoke to myself as if I were a daughter of God.

"Tracey, stop doing this to yourself. You know who God created you to be. You are strong. You've always been strong."

Even though I had softened, I'd allowed some things to pass that I usually would have stood up against. The core of me was still that bold, God-fearing woman. The woman who stood her ground. Who went to church. Who prayed with conviction. Who gave her all to God.

I remembered her.

I remembered the woman who spoke up, so I started speaking again. I remembered the woman who wasn't ashamed of her voice, so I used it. Yes, I had to dig deep. Yes, I had to revisit old wounds. But something had shifted. I had lost my mother. I had lost my father. I had lost my spouse. My children were grown. And in the silence of my home, with only my sweet dogs and the Lord, I realized I no longer cared what others thought.

I didn't owe anyone an explanation. I only answered to God. And He had already declared me worthy.

That's when it clicked. My trials weren't my shame. They were my testimony. The pain didn't aim to punish me. It was to prepare me. To give me a voice that could lift others. A light that could shine into someone else's darkness.

So I began to shift how I lived. I stopped apologizing for taking up space. I stopped walking small in rooms where God had given me important assignments. I started showing up with intention. I prayed differently. I praised louder. I walked taller. And every morning, I reminded myself that radiance is not a reward. It's a reflection of God's presence in my life.

I started to see things differently. Those weak moments I hated were proof that I needed God. And there is no shame in needing the One who created you. The One who strengthens you. The One who lifts your head.

I had to accept that perfection doesn't exist and I needed to stop chasing it. I decided that every single day I wake up is a blessing. A divine opportunity to radiate His goodness, to reflect His grace.
Radiance, for me, became a decision.

I chose to rise. I chose to smile at myself in the mirror and say, *"Good morning, beautiful. You're here for a reason."*

I chose to wear the yellow dress; a bold one I had believed was "too much." But you know what? I was stopped over and over again and told, *"You look beautiful. That color looks amazing on you. Your light is shining."*

I took a vacation by myself. I ate good food. I danced. I laughed. I talked to strangers. I praised God for the land, the people, and the beauty. I lived. I mean, really lived. I wore joy like a garment. I finally gave myself permission to shine without apology.

I decorated my home differently. I filled it with colors that made me feel alive. I started cooking meals for myself because I was worth the effort. I stopped waiting for someone else to encourage me. I started affirming myself in God's truth.

My pastor had given me a prayer to recite. And, although I had said it daily, I had not delved into the whole meaning of it. I began to declare it every day with purpose, joy, and gratitude. I had to let the words soak into my spirit. I had to remind myself: I am not ashamed. I am not forgotten. I am not done.

Wash me, cleanse me, purge me with hyssop and purify me, Lord. Forgive me for my sins, transgressions, and iniquities. Renew the right spirit within me and make me whole!

Create within me a pure contrite heart. I praise you in advance for the miracles and divine recovery you are about to reward me, my God. And I shall forever be grateful for the opportunity to call upon your Holy name! Amen!

That prayer became the foundation of my return to strength. But it wasn't just words; it was my restoration in motion. I said it when I felt weak. I said it when I needed to stand. And every time I spoke it, the Lord met me right where I was.

Additionally, I was reminded of the Prayer of Jabez.

"...Oh that you would bless me indeed and enlarge my territory! Let your hand be with me, and keep me from harm so that I will be free from pain."

After praying that restoration prayer from my pastor, I would follow it up with the words of Jabez. A cry not just for healing, but for purpose. A prayer that asked God to enlarge my territory, to walk with me in every place He assigned, to protect me from harm, and to prevent me from inadvertently harming others. It reminded me that my life wasn't just about survival; it was designed to expand. To grow. To walk in overflow. To serve. To help others. To testify. To direct others to the Lord.

God gave me a second chance. A third. A tenth. An infinite number of chances. And I finally said, *"No more wasting them."*

No more wasting time on what could have been. No more trying to explain myself to people who never had the capacity to understand my journey. No more dimming my light for people who are uncomfortable with my shine.

Now, I rise with intention. I put on clothes that reflect the joy I feel. I breathe deeply. I pray boldly. I walk freely. I dance even when there's no music. I laugh out loud even when I'm alone. I sit with my dogs and give thanks to God for peace. I journal with gratitude. I speak life.
Because when God shines on you, shame has no place to hide.

So this is me. Radiant. Reclaimed. Redeemed. I'm not ashamed of my story. I'm grateful for it.
And if you're reading this and still carrying shame, hear me: You don't have to carry it another day. You are beautiful. You are seen. You are worthy. You are radiant.

Let the shame fall off. Let the light come in. Because your shine is your testimony, and it's time to walk in it.

Guided Activity: Release the Weight

Supplies: A small stone(s) and a permanent marker.
1. Write a word on the stone(s) that represents your shame.
2. Hold it in your hand and speak aloud:

"This is no longer mine to carry. I lay it at the feet of Jesus."

3. Go outside and place the stone(s) somewhere permanent — a garden, a tree, a river — as a symbol that the burden is released.
4. Say aloud: *"I am free. I am forgiven. I am whole."*

Shame often feels invisible, but its weight is real. This activity invites you to name it, release it, and walk away lighter, because you were never purposed to carry what the Lord has already covered.

Study Questions for Reflection

1. What moments in your life have left you feeling ashamed or rejected?
2. Have you ever apologized for something that wasn't your fault?
3. In what ways has silence robbed you of healing?
4. How can you remind yourself daily of your identity in Christ?
5. What would it look like to walk completely free from shame?
6. What moment in your healing journey made you realize you no longer needed to apologize for your past or your pain?
7. How have you seen God begin to "enlarge your territory," whether emotionally, spiritually, or in purpose, since releasing shame?
8. What are three radiant truths about yourself that you can speak out loud every morning as a declaration of who you are in Christ?
9. How can your story of overcoming shame help someone else feel less alone and more seen? Are you willing to let your shine become someone else's guiding light?

Closing Prayer

God, thank You for not turning away from my pain. Thank You for loving me past my shame and calling me radiant even when I felt unworthy. Today, I lay down every burden You never meant for me to carry. I release guilt, regret, comparison, and self-condemnation. I rise in Your truth. I stand in Your grace. I declare that I am redeemed, restored, and radiant in Your name. From this day forward, I walk in freedom. In Jesus' name, Amen.

CHAPTER SIX
Undeliverable—Address No Longer Valid

Key Verse

"Forget the former things; do not dwell on the past. See, I am doing a new thing! Now it springs up; do you not perceive it?" — Isaiah 43:18–19

Opening Prayer

Heavenly Father, I come before You today with a heart open to healing. I release the burdens of my past and the addresses where my pain has lived. I invite You into my process. Help me understand what needs to be returned, what no longer serves me, and what You have already healed. May this chapter serve as a mirror that reflects truth, restoration, and forward movement. In Jesus' name, Amen.

The Power of Change and Forward Movement

There's something powerful about a piece of returned mail. That bold black stamp — **RETURN TO SENDER: UNDELIVERABLE, ADDRESS NO LONGER VALID.** It's more than just postal jargon. It's a declaration. A declaration that whoever lived there no longer does. A shift has taken place. The past has been vacated. A new residence has been claimed.

And if you're reading this chapter, you may be standing right there—somewhere between the place you used to live emotionally or spiritually and the unknown territory God is calling you to inhabit next. Perhaps it was a relationship that once defined you. A job title that gave you value. A community or identity that once fit like a glove, but now, it's too tight. It doesn't feel like home anymore.

Sometimes, God allows rejection to close the old address. Not as punishment, but as redirection. Not because you're broken, but because you're being preserved for something else.

What about the "Lie of Unfamiliarity?" Let's be honest. We romanticize the past. We remember how it made us feel in the good moments and forget how it made us shrink in the bad ones. But one of the most dangerous things you can do is camp out at the site of your last disappointment, hoping it might change. That maybe if you wait long enough, they'll come back, it'll get better, or you'll feel wanted again. But God's deliverance rarely takes place where you were once held captive. And His promises aren't found in areas marked "Return to Sender."

The Bible is full of those who moved forward when staying would have been easier. Joseph was betrayed by his brothers, falsely accused, and imprisoned. But in *Genesis 50:20*, he tells his brothers: *"You intended to harm me, but God intended it for good to accomplish what is now being done..."* Joseph didn't let betrayal stop him. He didn't return to the pit. He moved forward and embraced his role in a palace.

Ruth lost her husband and could've returned to her homeland. Still, she clung to Naomi and made a decision to walk forward into uncertainty. She didn't stay where her life had died. In Moab, her past ended. In Bethlehem, her future began.

Paul, once Saul, had every reason to live in shame. He had violently persecuted the early church. But after his encounter with Christ, he moved. He became a new man and walked with boldness. He didn't stay at the site of his shame. He preached from it.

Let's not sugarcoat it. Forward movement requires grief and grit. Leaving old places behind can be a painful experience. Rejection cuts. Silence from someone you once loved leaves bruises. The job that let you go. The church that closed its doors on you. The friend who disappeared. You might cry. You might want to go back. But here's the truth: if God allowed it to be labeled undeliverable, it's because He has somewhere else for you to go. Grieve it. Yes, honor the loss. But then, get up and go!

When God closes a door, don't stand there knocking. We've all done it; stood outside the doors of old seasons, knocking and hoping they'll let us back in. But God is saying, *"That was only for a time. The oil has run out. The grace has lifted."*

If a door is locked, it may not be the enemy keeping you out. Perhaps it's God guarding your destiny. Because the only thing worse than being rejected from the wrong room is being accepted into a place that was never designed to hold your growth.

Don't build a house in a hallway. It's tempting to settle in transition. It doesn't matter what you brought with you: a divorce, a layoff, a betrayal, or even the death of someone you loved deeply. You find yourself in a place that's neither here nor there. A space where the past has closed, but the future hasn't opened yet.

You start saying things like:
"At least I know how this feels."
"At least I had that for a little while."
"Maybe this is just where I'm meant to be for now."

But God never called you to live in limbo. Grief may visit, but it should never be allowed to build walls around you. Let me say it plainly: pain is a process, not a place. Transition is a tunnel, not a tomb.

I've lived in those hallways. Maybe not all at once, but over the years, I've visited plenty of them. After the divorce, yes. But also after unexpected losses. After friends who were once talking to me suddenly didn't know what to say. After cancer shook my body and my schedule, I was reminded that the familiar isn't always promised.

Even grief—genuine, legitimate, holy grief—can feel like rejection from life as you knew it. And it makes you wonder: *"Did I do something wrong? Why didn't life keep going the way it was?"*

But here's the truth. God is not punishing you. He's pruning you. And sometimes the branches He trims feel like everything you thought you needed to survive. But you're still here, not shrinking to fit inside the hallway.

Some losses leave you limping. I say, *"Walk forward, even if you limp."*

Whether it's rejection by people or simply the shift of life itself, the effect is the same. It shakes your stability.

The child who left home no longer calls the way they used to. The ministry you poured your heart into that eventually phased you out. The friend group that celebrated you when you were giving but ghosted you when you were grieving.

You start to wonder if something's wrong with you. Let me impart something to you. Nothing is wrong with your heart. Grief is not meant to live in every room it once entered. When you love deeply and lose deeply, it can feel like death even when it's simply a redirection.

And when someone passes away, you're left standing in a space that once echoed with their presence. And suddenly it's silent. You didn't get a vote. You didn't get a say. But now you're left to walk forward through the hallway of what was, into the unknown of what will be.

Rejection isn't always a person saying no. Sometimes it's life's way of letting you know that this is no longer for you. And that's where trust comes in. When God allows a door to close, even if it's not slammed shut by betrayal, He's still leading you.

You may not have all the answers. But you do have a promise: *"I will never leave you nor forsake you"* (Hebrews 13:5).

That includes hallways. That includes grief. That includes uncertainty. And that means there's no need to build a house in a place whose only purpose was to lead you to healing.

You've been stamped. Not with failure. Not with shame. But with this truth: **"This address is no longer valid. The woman I used to be doesn't live here anymore."** Let's move forward.

Steps to Freedom – Walking Boldly into the New

There comes a moment, after the ache of rejection and the fog of uncertainty, when the soul begins to rise again. Not all at once. Sometimes in whispers. Sometimes it stumbles. But there is a quiet, sacred resolve that says: I cannot stay here. That resolve is the beginning of freedom. It starts not with fireworks, but with a flicker. A decision to move forward, even if you're unsure of the way.

The first step toward freedom is acknowledging what was lost without letting it redefine who you are. It's honoring the truth of the wound while refusing to let it become your name. Whether you've lost a relationship, a dream, or a role that once defined you, your value hasn't changed. *Ecclesiastes* reminds us that there is a time to mourn, but mourning doesn't mean you stop being who you are. You are still whole, even in your hurting.

The next step is surrendering the need for closure. That longing for a final conversation, a mutual understanding, or even an apology can keep you chained to the past. But true healing doesn't always come with neat endings. Sometimes you have to close the chapter yourself. You don't need their explanation to find your peace. You only need to choose it. Freedom is your decision and does not need their permission.

From there, you begin to reclaim your identity. After rejection, there's a temptation to become who you think others want you to be, adjusting your voice, your light, your softness, and your truth. But your life was never to be edited. God made you whole, not in fragments.

Psalm 139 says you are *fearfully and wonderfully made*, and no rejection has the power to unmake what God already called good.

As you step further into freedom, you'll likely wrestle with comparison and regret. The enemy loves to replay the highlight reels of others and the bloopers of your past. But comparison is a thief, and regret is a weight. Isaiah tells us to forget the former things; not because they didn't matter, but because they are not your final destination. What you couldn't see was that God was already working for your good.

Loneliness may try to visit you in this new space. And it's in those quiet, hollow places that you may feel most vulnerable. Guard your heart. Loneliness is not a sign to return to what hurt you. It's a reminder to sit with God until you're full again. When your soul feels empty, resist the urge to fill it with something seasonal. Let God meet you in the silence.

One of the most courageous decisions you'll ever make is saying yes to the unknown. The unfamiliar path doesn't always come with clear signs or safe maps. But faith says yes anyway. Like Abraham, who walked away not knowing where he was going, you, too, are being invited into a new land, a new chapter, a new identity. Uncertainty isn't your enemy. It's your invitation to trust.

Finally, freedom is not just about what you know. It's about how you walk in it. You can declare it with your lips, but you must also live it with your life. Show up. Speak truth. Set boundaries. Rest. Begin again. Even if your steps are small and trembling, they still count. James reminds us that faith without works is dead. So walk. Limp if you must but keep moving. You are no longer waiting for the life you lost. You're partnering with a life that's still unfolding.

And as you continue this journey, ask yourself: *What am I still carrying that's weighing me down? What truths am I ready to walk in today?*

Your story didn't end at rejection. It began again. And with each step you take, you are reclaiming your freedom, your voice, and your purpose. One brave yes at a time.

Return to Sender: Hurdles to Horizons
Girl Godsip Series: Book 3

Guided Activity: "Lighten the Load"

You've spent enough time lingering in emotional hallways. Now it's time to forward your mail.

1. Take a blank sheet of paper and draw a line down the middle. On the left side, write everything that no longer has access to you. These may include:
    a. People or relationships that drained you
    b. Habits or coping mechanisms you've outgrown
    c. Labels, lies, or expectations that made you feel small
    d. Environments or mindsets that keep you bound

2. On the right side, write the truth of what you are forwarding in your life to:
    a. A healthier you
    b. A clear identity
    c. Purpose-filled relationships
    d. Peaceful boundaries
    e. New beginnings in Christ

3. Fold the paper and place it in an envelope.

4. On the front, write: "FORWARD TO: The Next Version of ME"

5. Say a prayer of release over the envelope. If possible, place it in your Bible or lay it at your church altar or a sacred place to you.

6. WALK AWAY LIGHTER. Let it be done. Trust that God has already marked it:

"DELIVERED. SIGNED. SEALED. HEALED."

Study Questions for Reflection

1. What past situation, relationship, or identity have I been stuck in for too long?
2. What is my emotional or spiritual "old address" that I need to leave behind?
3. Have I been waiting for closure from someone? If so, how has that affected my healing?
4. What lies about myself have I believed because of rejection or loss?
5. What comparison or regret do I need to release today?
6. When do I feel most tempted to settle for something that's no longer for me?
7. How can I guard my heart in this season of transition or loneliness?
8. What does walking forward by faith look like for me this week?
9. What promise from God do I need to hold onto more tightly than the pain I'm letting go?

Closing Prayer

God, I thank You for being a faithful Deliverer. The One who does not leave me stuck or stranded in yesterday. Thank You for closing every door that no longer serves my growth and gently guiding me toward the next version of myself. Help me to release what is no longer mine. Break every chain that keeps me emotionally parked in places You've already called me out of.

Teach me how to move. How to walk, even when I feel unsure. How to trust, even when the path looks unfamiliar. Strengthen my faith so that I don't settle in transitional spaces. Cover me with grace as I walk boldly into newness. I forward my life to You, God. Deliver me into purpose, into peace, and into divine alignment. In Jesus' name, Amen.

CHAPTER SEVEN
The Climb to Clarity

Key Verse

"Trust in the Lord with all your heart and lean not on your own understanding; in all your ways submit to him, and he will make your paths straight."
– Proverbs 3:5–6

Opening Prayer

Heavenly Father, open my eyes as I climb out of confusion and pain. Let every step I take toward clarity be guided by Your hand. When the path is steep and unknown, anchor me in Your love and peace. Help me to understand the lessons in every fall and to find healing in the climb. In Jesus' name, Amen.

Footsteps in the Forest – Conquering What Tried to Stop Me

The air was thick that morning in Costa Maya. The kind of density that presses against your chest and makes you question every decision that brought you to this moment. I was excited to take an excursion to see the Mayan Ruins; however, there was a small snare in the plan that I hadn't prepared for. I thought our big tour bus would park adjacent to the pyramids and we would simply hop off, be in awe, take photos, and hop back on board.

As our guide began speaking during the one-hour ride, he told us we would have a fantastic day, while handing out release forms, which were mandatory to complete. A release form? Why was this necessary?

The guide explained that there were many wild animals in the rain forest and that we could encounter one of these beauties along our hike. The following words pierced my soul: WILD ANIMALS, RAIN FOREST, and HIKE!

I'm not an outdoor person. I am allergic to most grasses, swell like crazy when I get bitten by a mosquito, and I don't want to get stung by a bee. I run away from lizards and cats, so wild animals were certainly out of the question. Additionally, it had been years since I had engaged in any sort of outdoor activity that involved sweating. Besides, I had just gotten my hairstylist to give me a style that would last the entire trip. But I thought, *"I'm already on the bus, so there's no turning back now."*

I completed the form and politely handed it back to our guide, all the while psyching myself out about what was ahead. Surely it couldn't be as bad as the sheer panic I felt inside. The bus came to a halt, and the guide welcomed us to our destination. I almost passed out from sheer anxiety about what was to come. At that moment, I decided it would be essentially mind over matter. I wouldn't be outdone and would push myself to do my best.

I stood at the edge of a rainforest and followed my small group down the entry trail. All I could hear was the sound of my heartbeat, pounding out a rhythm of fear and resistance. At first, it was frightening. However, as I continued walking, I became less worried and began to notice the beauty surrounding me. There were amazingly beautiful and colorful plants I'd never seen before, and lush greenery spanning as far as I could see.

We walked and walked, stopping only occasionally for our guide to point out interesting sites along the way. At times, I thought I was going to pass out from the heat and humidity, but each time I felt this way, I refused to give up. I kept pushing, and eventually the trek got a little easier.

I was sweating so much that it felt as though I had walked through a sprinkler. I was tired, sweaty, and exhausted, but then we reached a fork. We chose the path to the right, and there it was. I was staring at an ancient Mayan pyramid that seemed to have been built to reach heaven itself. The guide smiled as he introduced us to this astounding spectacle. There were remnants of the pyramids in the area. Still, this one had been excavated, restored, and was now a resilient reminder of a great civilization existing just after the turn of the century. We took pictures and continued walking down the next path.

We walked for a short time until we happened upon another impressive pyramid. This time, the guide encouraged us to climb the steep steps to the top. He told us to be careful as some steps were very narrow and difficult to manage. The walls were jagged in some places, not offering a stable place to hold onto in the event you lose your balance. He went on to say that EMS had been dispatched the day before for a woman who was seriously injured when she fell attempting to make the same climb he had just offered us. Well, that was enough for me.

Everything in me wanted to stay at the bottom. To say *no thank you* and let others make the climb while I sat safely on the ground. But something deeper—sacred—whispered, *"This climb is not about them. It's about you."*

It wasn't about a tourist experience. It was about trusting God to take me beyond my fear. It was about proving to myself that I was not going to die at the base of something I was born to overcome. I handed my bag to the guide, and he graciously agreed to hold it while I attempted to scale the giant fixture.

Each step upward felt like a war. The uneven stones beneath my feet echoed the emotional terrain I'd been walking for months: fear of the unknown, fear of being alone, and fear that I didn't have what it took. But with every careful step, I heard God whisper, *"I am with you. I go before you."*

And the Word came to life: *Be strong and courageous. Do not be afraid or terrified... for the Lord your God goes with you; he will never leave you nor forsake you. (Deuteronomy 31:6).*

The climb wasn't just physical. It was spiritual. It was emotional. It was generational. I felt the weight of every no I'd ever heard. Every door slammed. Every identity crisis. Every time I thought I had to shrink to be accepted. And I carried it all in my breath, in my legs, in my tears.

But I climbed.

I didn't climb like a warrior. I climbed like a woman who was tired but still willing. I climbed like a woman who wasn't sure if she would make it, but knew she couldn't stay where she was. I paused often. I cried. I prayed. I wanted to quit more than once. But the Spirit of God was stronger than the fear that taunted me.

About halfway up, my muscles started trembling. Not from exertion, but from memory. Memories of all the emotional climbs I'd made previously: leaving behind a marriage that no longer held life, walking into new leadership roles when I felt inadequate, starting a business while battling uncertainty, saying yes to life after loss. These climbs didn't leave physical bruises, but they stretched me, shaped me, and, sometimes, scarred me.

I remembered a moment, not long before this trip, when I sat on the edge of my bed staring at a stack of unopened mail. Bills. Medical updates. Reminders of what I had lost and what I had yet to face. I felt frozen. Like life was calling me to move, but I couldn't get my feet to follow. That climb in the rainforest felt eerily familiar. That same tension between fear and faith. That same invitation to move despite everything.

I thought about every time I had tried to talk myself out of believing again. Out of dreaming again. Out of starting again. The enemy doesn't always roar. Sometimes he instills just enough doubt to make you question what God already told you. But with every step, I silenced the noise with worship.

And still, I kept going. Not quickly. Not perfectly. But forward. Because something inside of me knew that there was clarity at the top. That God doesn't call us to climb just to punish us. He calls us higher because there are things you can only see when you've left the fog of fear behind.

When I reached the summit, I stood in silence. The rainforest stretched out endlessly below me. The sounds of the jungle now seemed peaceful, rather than threatening. The view wasn't just scenic, it was sacred. And in that moment, I felt something shift inside me. I wasn't just a woman who survived something hard. I was a woman who conquered it. And the clarity I received wasn't about the moment. It was about my life.

And when I reached the top, I saw the most beautiful sight that was completely invisible from ground level. There was a grassy pasture at the top with two other pyramids. I would have missed the beauty lying high above if I had just waited and wallowed at the bottom. A whole new world was at the top, and I almost missed it.

This is how I felt about my personal life in that moment. I was missing the beauty of a full life because I wasn't willing to climb. I was staying on ground level, and that's precisely what I had reaped: a ground-level life. Now, it was time for me to go higher and consciously climb.

That pyramid became a symbol. A holy metaphor. Every fear I had faced. Every hurt I held. Every label I had been given. They all tried to stop me, but they didn't succeed. They didn't have the final word. *Psalm 18:33* says, *"He makes my feet like the feet of a deer; he causes me to stand on the heights."*

And truly, God had steadied me. Positioned me. Elevated me, not above others, but above the mindset that once kept me bound.

I didn't just gain perspective. I regained power. I began to understand that clarity doesn't always arrive in thunder. Sometimes it comes in stillness. In breath. In perspective. When you look down from the place you thought you'd never reach and realize you are no longer who you were when you started. The climb changed me. God used the height to heal me. And the woman standing here now? She has a new name: Free!

I climbed that pyramid with trembling knees. But I descended with steady feet and a heart full of praise. The jungle didn't defeat me. The fear didn't define me. The climb became my testimony.

Since that day, whenever I'm met with something that feels insurmountable—a diagnosis, a delay, a betrayal—I close my eyes and go back to the forest. I remind myself; I've climbed before. I can climb again. And what tried to stop me then doesn't stand a chance against the God who strengthens me now.

So if you're facing a climb of your own—spiritual, emotional, relational—understand this: The height may scare you, but the view is worth it. And God? He never wastes a single step. And neither will you.

Don't Descend for the Familiar – Hold the Vision Higher Than Fear—Grateful for the Glimpse

There's something sacred about reaching the top, but there's something even more powerful about what you do after you come down.

When I returned to ground level from my trek up the pyramid, the terrain hadn't changed. The humidity was still heavy. The jungle sounds still echoed. The ground was still uneven. But something in me had shifted. I did not descend the same woman who had started at the base.

What I experienced at the summit wasn't permanent elevation. It was a sacred glimpse. A moment where clarity pierced through the fog and reminded me that I didn't have to live scared—that I didn't have to walk around reacting to life like I was still wounded. I had seen what clarity looked like. And once you've seen it, you can't go back to blurry.

When I had to re-enter my reality, the same relationships, the same unanswered questions, and the same fears waiting to creep in again, but they didn't grip me in the same way. Why? Because I had seen what was possible. God had given me a peek. A holy preview of what life could feel like when fear doesn't sit in the driver's seat.

Many of us pray to God for unclouded vision. And, when He gives it to us, that mountaintop glimpse, we think it's supposed to be permanent. It's not. Sometimes clarity is a moment of light, so you know which direction to go. Sometimes it's a breath of peace so you remember who you are. But it's always meant to empower you, not paralyze you, in perfection.

I came down from that pyramid with a new mindset. Not a perfect one. Not a finished one. But a steadier one. The kind of mindset that says, I might still face hard things, but now I face them from a place of insight, not intimidation. I didn't need every answer. I just needed a clear step, a reason to keep moving.

That's the real beauty of clarity; it doesn't remove the unknown. It just gives you the confidence to walk into it. I've faced decisions since that climb that would've sent me spiraling in the past. But something changed when I realized that fear doesn't have the final word. The final word belongs to God.

The danger after experiencing clarity is returning to what's familiar simply because it's comfortable. You can't unsee what you've seen. You can't unlearn peace. And yet, the temptation to go back to small thinking, to fear-based patterns, to people who don't require your growth is real. That's why the title of this section matters. Don't descend toward the familiar.

It takes discipline to carry vision back down the mountain and apply it in the valley. It takes surrender to walk into what God showed you without demanding that everyone else understand it. Some won't. Some never will. But that doesn't make the vision any less real.

There were nights after that trip when I still cried. There were days I still doubted. But I prayed differently. I moved differently. I made decisions from a place of wholeness, not desperation. And that alone was evidence that the climb had done something inside me that comfort never could.

God had shown me a future version of myself. He had pulled back the curtain for just a moment, enough for me to see that peace was possible. That confidence could grow. That healing was within reach. And that was all I needed to keep walking forward, even when the road was unfamiliar.

If you've been given a glimpse of clarity, don't let it go. Write it down. Pray over it. Revisit it in hard times. Let it be your anchor. *Habakkuk 2:2* reminds us to write the vision and make it plain, because there will be days when you'll need to reread what God already revealed.

And when life starts to press in again, when the enemy tries to blur your lens with fear and confusion, go back in your spirit to the place of clarity. Remind yourself *"I've seen the top. I've seen who I can be. I've seen what it feels like to walk unafraid. And no matter what I face, I will hold that vision higher than fear."*

You may not be on a physical pyramid, but you are climbing. You are ascending. You are stepping out of confusion and into purpose. And once you see who you are in the light, you'll never again feel comfortable in the dark.

Here's what clarity does: it doesn't erase the circumstances; it reorients you within them. That's what happened when I climbed down from the pyramid. I was going back into the same situation, the same unresolved issues, the same external mess. But I wasn't carrying the same fear. I wasn't carrying the same doubt. The woman who descended had seen something. And that glimpse changed everything.

It was as if God had pulled back the veil for just a moment, allowing me to see what was possible, not just in the world, but within myself. And that glance gave me courage. Because sometimes, the only thing keeping us from moving forward is the mystery of what's ahead. But if we could just have a peek—a glimpse—we wouldn't be so afraid.

That's what that climb was. It was as if God were giving me a preview. A holy sneak peek of peace. Of what life could feel like on the other side of fear. It didn't mean I'd live in permanent clarity. It didn't mean the fog wouldn't try to return. But now I had seen the light, and that light would guide me forward.

After I came down from the climb, I prayed in a different way. I didn't ask for dramatic breakthroughs or thunderous change. I asked for steady feet. For a fresh vision. For the grace to keep walking with peace—even when peace didn't always surround me. And slowly, steadily, it came. One prayer at a time. One moment of courage at a time.

Letting go of what was holding me back wasn't one big, bold act. It was daily. It was quiet. It was private. But it was monumental. Because for the first time, I didn't need external validation to feel strong. I didn't need all the answers to feel safe. I had clarity. And that glimpse was enough to anchor me.

You don't have to stay on the mountaintop to live like you've been there. You have to remember what you saw. You have to carry that vision back into the ordinary. Let it transform how you walk through your home, how you respond to frustration, and how you speak to your reflection. That's what walking in clarity looks like.

And even now, when life gets noisy or the path gets dark, I go back in my spirit to that moment. That climb. That breakthrough. I remind myself: You've seen what peace looks like. You've touched the edge of clarity. You've glimpsed at who you really are. Don't descend for the familiar. Don't bow to fear. Keep walking forward. Clarity is waiting.

Guided Activity: The Glimpse That Guides Me

Sometimes God doesn't change the whole picture. He gives you a glimpse so you can change how you walk in it.

Instructions:
Draw or list your "climb."
On a blank sheet of paper, sketch or write out the journey you've been climbing.
- What fears did you face at the bottom?
- What emotions showed up halfway?
- What clarity did you find at the top?

At the summit, write what you saw.
1. Peace. Strength. Identity. Courage. Freedom. Write it boldly in the center. This is your vision. This is your glimpse.

Draw a path leading down.
On that path, write the words or truths you need to carry back down with you:
- I am no longer afraid of the unknown.
- I've seen who I really am.
- I can live with peace even in messy places.

Keep the paper in your journal or Bible.
1. On days when you feel like you're slipping back into old patterns, revisit the vision. Let that glimpse remind you how far you've come.

Study Questions for Reflection

1. What does "the climb" represent in this season of your life?
2. What fears did you face along the way, and how did God strengthen you?
3. What did you glimpse at the "top" about God, yourself, or your future?
4. What parts of you changed as a result of seeing that vision?
5. What situations in your life stayed the same, even after your internal shift?
6. How do you guard the clarity gained when familiar patterns try to pull you back?
7. Have you been tempted to descend back into the familiar? Why?
8. What spiritual truths can you carry with yourself on the path forward?
9. How can you daily align your steps with the glimpse God gave you?

Closing Prayer

God, thank You for giving me a glimpse. A glimpse of peace, of purpose, of who I really am in You. Thank You for letting me see what life looks like when fear doesn't win. I know I can't always live on the mountaintop, but I can carry with me what I saw in that moment. Help me to hold onto the vision You gave me. When the path gets muddy or the air gets thick, remind me of the summit. Remind me that I am changed. I am called. I am equipped to walk forward boldly, faithfully, and free. Let me never descend for the familiar. Let me never exchange my clarity for comfort. Let me keep moving toward the woman You showed me I could be. In Jesus' name, Amen.

CHAPTER EIGHT
Rebuilding After Rejection

Key Verse

"They will rebuild the ancient ruins and restore the places long devastated; they will renew the ruined cities that have been devastated for generations.."
— Isaiah 61:4

Opening Prayer

Father, I surrender the ruins of rejection into Your hands. Please teach me how to rebuild on a firm foundation. Guide me as I rise from the ashes—not on my own strength, but in Yours. Remind me daily that I am not what I lost. I am who You are restoring. In Jesus' name, Amen.

When the Dust Settles – Finding Strength in the Stillness

When the dust settles, everything looks different, not because the landscape has changed, but because you have. You come down off the climb, off the high place where God gave you a glimpse, and your feet hit the familiar ground again. But this time, you're carrying clarity.

The noise that once shook you no longer commands your attention. The silence that once haunted you now feels holy. This is not the silence of absence. It's the stillness of alignment. And in that stillness, you realize you are standing on something solid. Something sacred. Peace.

There was a time when stillness felt like punishment. Like exile. Like you had been left behind or forgotten. But now? It feels like rest. It feels like the pause before the blueprint is revealed. It feels like God saying, *"You don't have to run anymore."* Psalm 40:2 says, *"He lifted me out of the slimy pit… he set my feet on a rock and gave me a firm place to stand."* That is the power of stillness after the storm. It's not a weakness. It's recovery.

Stillness becomes your sanctuary. It becomes a sign that you are no longer living from trauma, but from trust. That you no longer need constant motion to validate your worth. That you can sit in the presence of God and know that you are already loved, already whole, already enough.

When you've spent years reacting to rejection, you begin to mistake chaos for normal. You crave movement, noise, emotional highs and lows, anything that proves you're still needed, still seen, still surviving. But once you've climbed and glimpsed clarity, you realize that survival is no longer the goal. Healing is. Stability is. Peace is.

And now that the dust has settled, you get to see what's still standing. You get to walk through the ruins and recognize that not all of it was designed to last. The pieces that remain? Those are the pieces that matter. Those are the truths from which you will rebuild.

This is your moment of holy inventory. You're not just sweeping up brokenness. You're choosing what gets to come with you into the next season. You're holding every shattered piece up to the light and asking, *"Does this serve who I am now?"*

And if it doesn't, you bless it, release it, and let it fall away.

Stillness doesn't mean nothing is happening. It means the foundation is being prepared, deep beneath the surface, God is settling the soil of your identity. He's quieting the lies. He's strengthening the ground. Because when you start building again, it won't be because of pain. It will be on the truth.

You start to see it—the beauty in simplicity. The holiness in a quiet morning. The power in saying no. The healing in saying yes to rest. This is what the climb prepared you for: the vision to see your life not as it used to be, but as it could become.

You realize the version of you that begged for attention and hustled for worth no longer lives here. The woman who doubted her voice, who played small to make others comfortable, and feared being alone, has been buried in the dust. And what rises now is something holy.

And the most victorious part of all? You're not desperate anymore. You're not begging for validation. You're not waiting to be chosen. You know who you are. You've walked with fear and kept going. You've seen the top and returned with wisdom. You are rebuilding from a place of peace, not panic.

Stillness doesn't mean absence. It means access. Access to God's whisper. Access to your intuition. Access to grace. For the first time, you're not rushing to fill silence; you're listening inside of it. You're hearing God in the spaces where fear used to speak. Let that settle in: the very stillness that once made you feel abandoned has now become evidence that God is near. Not loud. Not forceful. But faithful. Present. Holding you steady in the pause between what was and what will be.

The most powerful part of this rebuilding isn't the outcome. It's the mindset. You've come down from that mountain, and you didn't come empty-handed. You brought perspective. You brought discernment. You brought boundaries. And now you build not for applause, but for alignment.

In this stillness, God is teaching you to lay bricks of truth. To frame your thoughts with peace. To install windows of wisdom and doors of discernment. Everything you're rebuilding now is shaped by what you saw in that glimpse, and you won't forget it. Your peace is proof of progress. Your stillness is sacred. And when the dust settles, don't rush to rebuild everything at once. Breathe. Stand in the strength of who you've become. And let God show you what's next—brick by holy brick.

Blueprints and Broken Pieces – Building What Rejection Tried to Destroy

Rebuilding is not a glamorous process. It's not the beautiful reveal you see at the end of a renovation show. It's the debris, dust in your lungs, and ache in your back. And that's what healing often looks like. It's sacred, but it's not always pretty. When you come down from the mountain of clarity and your feet hit the ground, what's next is rebuilding. But this time, you're not building from broken identity; you're building from truth. This is your blueprint season.

Every woman who has been rejected has to face this moment. When she looks around at the damage and decides the broken pieces won't be wasted. The moment when she opens her hands and says, *"God, here is everything left behind. Everything I lost. Everything I thought I couldn't live without. Show me what to do with it."*

And God, in His grace, responds not with shame but with strategy. He whispers, *"Let's build."* Isaiah 61:3–4 says, *They will rebuild the ancient ruins and restore the places long devastated.*

That's what this chapter is about. You, standing in the ruins with a hammer in one hand and a prayer in the other.

There were times I thought I was starting over, but really, I was being invited to go deeper. After the divorce. After the diagnosis. After the friendships faded, I thought the rejection was the end, but God was showing me the beginning.

I started picking up broken pieces. Not to relive the pain, but to find the materials for my healing. Every time I cried out in prayer, every time I journaled through the hurt, every time I took a step toward purpose, I was sketching the lines of a new structure. A life that will not crumble when the next storm hits.

I stopped trying to rebuild what was and started asking God to show me what could be because the old foundation wasn't strong enough to hold what He had in store for me. You see, the old foundation was built on people's approval. On performance. On perfectionism. It had to be torn down. And if that's where you are right now, don't be afraid of the demolition. God never destroys without the intention to rebuild.

Here's what I learned: rejection isn't the absence of purpose. It's an invitation to build it. And every time you feel like something is being taken from you, it's possible that God is just clearing the way and making space for something solid. Something lasting.

I had to redefine what I deserved, not in a prideful, self-centered way, but in a healed, holy way. I realized that just because something was available didn't mean it was aligned. That just because something was familiar didn't mean it was for me. Rejection made me doubt my value. But healing helped me rewrite the blueprint. And now I build with boundaries. I build with clarity. I create with a God-given sense of worth.

Rebuilding means laying down the bricks one by one. Thoughtfully. Intentionally. And yes, it's tempting to rush the process. To want the house completed, the life restored, the heart made whole overnight. However, what I've come to understand is that sacred work is, in fact, slow work. The strongest structures are those that were installed correctly beneath the surface over time. Every brick I laid came from a decision to believe differently. To live differently. To think differently. I laid bricks with scriptures. With affirmations. With quiet mornings of worship and long nights of therapy. I let God rebuild me from the inside out.

You don't look like your rejection. That's the power of rebuilding. When people see the finished work, they won't believe the way you began. They won't understand what it costs you to rise again. But you'll know. You'll know what it meant to stand in the ruins and choose to rebuild anyway.

And perhaps the most empowering thing is learning how to help someone else. Healed women become architects for others. We don't just rebuild for ourselves; we show the next woman that it's possible. That which was torn down can be restored. That what was thrown away can be repurposed. Those broken pieces don't mean a broken future. So pick up the pieces, even if your hands still shake. Unroll the blueprint, even if your vision is still unclear. Start again, not despite rejection, but because of it, because rejection tried to destroy you. And you're still here. Still building. Still becoming.

Guided Activity: Rebuild With Intention

Sometimes the most powerful thing you can do is pick up the broken pieces and begin again with intention, with clarity, and with God as your architect.

This activity is a sacred blueprint for your next season.

Instructions:
1. On a blank sheet of paper, draw a house or building structure as simply or creatively as you'd like.

- At the base, label the FOUNDATION. Here, write three core truths you are choosing to believe about yourself and God.

- On the walls, write new BOUNDARIES or VALUES you are putting in place (i.e., "I don't accept emotional crumbs" or "I honor my healing pace").

- In the rooms, write your new priorities (e.g., peace, purpose, rest, spiritual growth).

- Above the structure, write a SCRIPTURE or PHRASE that will be your banner as you build (i.e., *Isaiah 61:3-4, I am rebuilding in truth*).

2. Around the blueprint, write the broken pieces you are choosing to repurpose and not discard. These may be past experiences, lessons, or even tears. These are the pieces God will use.

3. Pray over the entire image. Dedicate this space, this season, this sacred construction to the God who makes all things new.

Keep your blueprint visible as a reminder: you are building something worthy, brick by holy brick.

Study Questions for Reflection

1. What truths has God shown you in the stillness that you can now build on?
2. What parts of your old life or mindset no longer align with who you are becoming?
3. What does peace look like to you now, and how do you protect it daily?
4. How has rejection shaped your view of worth, and what truth replaces that lie?
5. What broken pieces do you now see as tools, not trash?
6. What boundaries do you need in place as you rebuild from a place of healing?
7. Who are you becoming as you move forward in this new construction season?
8. What is one brave step you can take this week toward the life God is helping you build?
9. What scripture can you lean on as your foundation during moments of doubt or fatigue?

Closing Prayer

God, thank You for not leaving me in the rubble. Thank You for steadying me when I could only see brokenness, and for giving me a glimpse of what's still possible. Help me to rebuild with intention, guided by Your Spirit, not by my fear. Please show me what to release and what to repurpose. Let me build from truth, not trauma. From wisdom, not wounds. Be my architect. Be my blueprint. Be the strength behind every brick I lay. When the process feels slow, remind me that sacred work takes time. When I feel tempted to rebuild what was, remind me You are doing a new thing. I trust You with my broken pieces. I believe You will use them for beauty. In Jesus' name, Amen.

CHAPTER NINE
Rediscovering Your Roots, Reclaiming Your Identity

Key Verse

"Stand at the crossroads and look; ask for the ancient paths, ask where the good way is, and walk in it, and you will find rest for your souls."
—*Jeremiah 6:16*

Opening Prayer

Heavenly Father, thank You for the roots that run deep beneath my story; the threads of heritage, faith, and resilience that have been woven through generations. I honor the people who came before me, those who walked long roads and crossed waters so that I could stand here today. Open my heart to rediscover the beauty of my identity, not just through my ancestors but through who I am in You. Please help me reclaim every part of myself that I've lost through rejection or pain. Anchor me in the truth that I am fearfully and wonderfully made, planted in purpose, and designed for your glory. In Jesus' name, Amen.

Rediscovering My Roots

There are moments in life when God allows you to experience something that pulls on a hidden thread of your soul, something that stirs an ancient connection you didn't even realize was there. My trip to Belize was one of those moments. I wasn't expecting a spiritual awakening or even a sense of homecoming. I simply thought I was going to see another country, take in the sights, taste the food, and enjoy a little time away. But God had other plans for me on that trip. He was ready to show me something about who I am, something about where I came from, and something about how deeply He has woven my life together.

When I stepped off the tour bus in Belize, I couldn't shake the feeling that I'd been there before. It was a strange sensation, almost as if my spirit recognized the land before my mind did. As we took in the sights and sounds, a quiet sense of knowing settled over me. The air felt familiar, the smiles of the people felt like home, and even the rhythm of the music seemed to beat in time with something inside of me.

Our phenomenal tour guide, Shelly, began explaining the history of the four primary cultures in Belize. I listened attentively, learned a great deal, and was intrigued by the rich history of this country. She spoke about the Maya, Mestizo, and Garifuna heritage. Each civilization was fascinating, and learning about their culture, dances, and cuisine was absolutely divine.

But then our guide began to speak about a fourth culture, and my ears perked up. My heart became full for no apparent reason. The guide started to tell us about the Belizean Creoles. How they came to be, how they settled along the coastlines, and how they fought to preserve their identity through language, food, and traditions.

I believed all Creole people were a blending of the races into a beautiful people in Louisiana in the United States of America. I was in awe hearing the stories of these people. Was it because my family history is steeped deeply in the Creole culture of Louisiana? Who were these new people with my family's cultural name?

With every word she spoke, I felt as though she was describing my family back in Louisiana. The similarities were undeniable. The dishes they cooked, the seasonings they used, and the music they danced to all mirrored my heritage and where I grew up.

Sometimes, when we face rejection and life's battles, we lose pieces of ourselves. It's as though we're walking around with holes in our identity, trying to remember who we were before life's blows knocked us down. That's why so many people search their family histories or take DNA identity tests. They're not just looking for names or percentages of ancestry; they're looking for themselves. Can discovering your legacy truly be a healing experience? That day in Belize, I realized I was doing the same thing without realizing it. I wasn't just on a tour; I was on a journey back to myself.

As I sat in a small, simple Belizean restaurant, the aromas of the food drifting through the air made me feel as though I was sitting at my grandmother's kitchen table. The warmth, the laughter, and the flavors were all there. I could almost hear my grandmother's voice calling me to come sit down and eat.

And I thought, isn't this what healing feels like? Healing isn't just about moving past pain; it's about finding the pieces of yourself that you thought were lost and bringing them home.

On that day, I found a connection that can never be broken. Belize is a beautiful country, but it is also deeply marked by poverty. The streets were not glamorous, the houses were simple, and life there was clearly not easy. Yet the people I met carried a sense of warmth and resilience that felt so familiar. It reminded me of my own family and the generations that came before me. People who didn't have much by the world's standards but had an abundance of love, grit, and faith. There was a peace that surpassed any I had felt previously. I hope to return to Belize in the near future for a more extended stay. Perhaps I will build a vacation home or establish a second home there. Who knows? I'll leave that part up to God.

As I looked around, I thought about the generations of Creole families who had lived in both Louisiana and Belize. They endured slavery, colonization, and displacement. Yet they built families, raised children, and passed down traditions that still live on today. And I realized that I am part of that same legacy.

Creole culture is a blending of African, European, and Caribbean influences. It's a culture born out of both pain and resilience, of both suffering and survival. And isn't that how many of us live? We are a mixture of the things that tried to break us and the strength that kept us standing.

When I think about my own life, I see a similar blending. I see the strength of my ancestors mixed with the grace of God. I see the hurt I've endured mixed with the healing that's still unfolding. I see the moments of rejection combined with the redemption that God has brought through every chapter of my story.

Sometimes, when life has rejected you, when jobs have let you go, when people have walked away, or when circumstances have left you feeling empty, remembering where you come from is like drinking from a well that never runs dry. It nourishes you. It reminds you that you are not just a random accident. You are part of a story that started long before you were born, and that story is still being written.

The most beautiful part of all this is knowing that God has been in every detail of my story, even before I was aware of it. *Acts 17:26* says that God *"marked out their appointed times in history and the boundaries of their lands."* When I think about that verse, I imagine God setting my family's story into motion and placing my ancestors in Louisiana, weaving in that rich Creole heritage, and planting within me a connection that would one day stretch across the ocean to Belize.

And just as God planned the boundaries of their lands, He has planned the boundaries of my life. He knew that I would one day stand in Belize and feel this sense of homecoming. He knew that I would feel a piece of my identity click into place in that moment. That realization humbled me. God doesn't just care about the big moments in our lives. He cares about the details. He cared enough to show me that even when I feel disconnected or rejected, I am still part of something bigger.

As I sat in Belize, eating the food and listening to music, I felt an unexpected peace. It was as though God was whispering, *"See? You're not lost. You're not alone. You are part of something sacred and beautiful."*

It was more than just learning about history. It was about reclaiming a piece of myself that I didn't even know was lost. And in that moment, I realized that heritage isn't just about where you come from; it's about where you belong.

Yes, I am part of this rich Creole heritage. But more than that, I belong to God. And just as I reconnected with my earthly roots in Belize, I have also been reconnecting with my spiritual roots through this journey of writing and healing.

The same peace I felt in Belize, the same comfort of feeling at home, is the peace I feel when I lean into my relationship with God. It's the peace that comes from understanding that He knew my lineage before I was ever born. He knows my DNA, my ancestors, my pain, my purpose, and my future. Belize reminded me that I have a heritage of resilience and faith. And that inheritance is not just in my bloodline, it's in my spirit!

Reclaiming My Identity

When I came home from my trip, I felt like a new person. The journey gave me more than just beautiful memories. It gave me a missing piece of myself. Rediscovering my roots awakened something deep within me. Still, it also reminded me that while roots provide us with history, identity is what we choose to reclaim and live out every single day. I returned with a renewed sense of purpose. I realized I have work to do, a calling to answer, and a life that cannot be lived halfway. And I cannot allow anyone—or anything—to stand in my way.

Before I left for my trip, I carried so many labels. I was the ex-wife, the mother, the nurse, the author, the veteran, the administrator, the president, the founder, the neighbor, the friend. Each of these roles came with expectations, demands, and responsibilities. But when I returned, I chose to wear just one label: child of God! Daughter of my amazing Father. I realized that every other label was temporary and earthly but being God's daughter is eternal. That is who I am above all else.

I've never been a fan of labels. As a child, they always made me uncomfortable. My mother, as incredible as she was, came with a shadow of expectations. She was a trailblazer, a true pioneer, and one of the first African American teachers to integrate a white school. She became an assistant principal, a principal, an assistant superintendent, and she founded the breast cancer organization I still lead today. My mother was a leader in every sense of the word. She set the bar high, and I was proud of her. But I also often felt invisible under her legacy.

When I attended the same high school where my mother was the assistant principal, it became more challenging. I couldn't walk down the hall without someone identifying me by her name. Inside, I wanted to scream, *"Hi, my name is Tracey!"* I wanted people to see me, not just her reflection. It wasn't my mother's fault, but as a child, I felt my identity was hidden beneath her accomplishments. Sometimes, I even rebelled just to prove I was my own person.

Looking back now, I see how much that experience shaped me. For years, I unknowingly let labels define my worth. I let other people's expectations, opinions, and judgments determine who I thought I was supposed to be. Rejection only made it worse. Rejection can rob you of so much. It can silence you, make you question your worth, and cause you to forget your own name. But God never called me to live under anyone else's label. He gave me my own.

Today, my label is simple: I am the one God chose. I am the one God loves. I am the one God redeemed and restored. And that is enough. Through every pain, every trial, and every moment of rejection, I've learned that God is the only one who can define my value. My identity doesn't come from the world. It comes from Him.

How many of us have lived our lives under labels given by other people? Maybe someone called you a failure, unworthy, or unlovable. Maybe someone defined you by a mistake you made or a season of your life. But you are not what they say you are. Your identity is declared by the One who created you.

God's Word says we are *"fearfully and wonderfully made" (Psalm 139:14)*. That is our heritage. That is our identity. It's not something we stumble upon. It's something we boldly declare. We speak it, we live it, and we refuse to let rejection or the opinions of others strip it away.

Since my travels, I've learned to find joy and confidence in being alone. I am not lonely because I know God is with me. I've rediscovered hobbies and passions that bring joy to my life. I've embraced the calling that God has placed on my heart, the one that existed before the pain tried to bury it. Reclaiming my identity has been about reawakening the true me. The Tracey that God envisioned long before I took my first breath.

When we reconnect with who we are in God, we find a wholeness that nothing else can give. For me, it has been a beautiful blending of my earthly roots, my Creole heritage, and my spiritual roots as God's daughter. My identity is not only inherited through my family line, but also divinely destined and purposed by God. And with that kind of foundation, how can I fail?

Guided Activity: Reclaim Your Voice

Take a sheet of paper and write down every label you feel the world has placed on you—both the good and the bad. Include roles, titles, and even the negative names you've been called. Once you've written the list, take a bold marker and write across the top: "I AM A CHILD OF GOD."

Spend five minutes in quiet reflection, asking God to reveal how He sees you. On the back of the paper, write down five new declarations about your identity that are rooted in God's Word.

I am chosen.
I am loved.
I am redeemed.
I am enough.
I am fearfully and wonderfully made.

Study Questions for Reflection

1. What labels have you been carrying that don't truly define you?
2. How has rejection or pain caused you to forget your actual identity?
3. When you think of your heritage, what strengths and values do you carry forward from your ancestors?
4. What role has God played in shaping your identity?
5. How does it feel to think of yourself primarily as a child of God rather than by your titles or roles?
6. What hobbies, passions, or dreams have you reclaimed since shedding old labels?
7. What Scripture speaks most deeply to your sense of identity in Christ?
8. How can you boldly declare your identity this week in a way that aligns with God's purpose for your life?
9. What steps can you take to ensure your voice and story are not silenced by rejection?

Closing Prayer

Father, thank You for reminding me that my worth is not tied to labels or the opinions of others. Thank You for my heritage, which You have given me, and the identity I have in You. Help me to release every false name and embrace the truth of who I am: chosen, loved, redeemed, and purposed by You. Teach me to walk boldly in this identity, to reclaim my voice, and to live out the calling You have placed on my life. In Jesus' name, Amen.

CHAPTER TEN
Dignity in the Departure

Key Verse

"The Lord will fight for you; you need only to be still." – Exodus 14:14

Opening Prayer

Lord, teach me to walk away with grace, even when I am misunderstood, rejected, or wronged. Remind me that I do not have to fight every battle with my own strength. Help me to trust that You see the truth, and that You are my vindicator. Teach me to embrace mystery, to find dignity in silence, and to leave space for You to work. In Jesus' name, Amen.

Leaving Something for the Imagination

There is an unshakable strength in learning when to depart gracefully, knowing when to hold your peace, and allowing God to speak on your behalf. *Exodus 14:14* says, *"The Lord will fight for you; you need only to be still."*

That verse has become a reminder that silence does not mean weakness and departure does not mean defeat. Sometimes our quiet exit speaks louder than any argument or explanation ever could.

Growing up, I remember my grandmother saying, *"You've got to leave something for the imagination."*

Of course, she was referring to young girls leaving home scantily dressed, but it still exudes the same thought. Everything does not have to be placed in the forefront. I began to understand that leaving something unsaid is not about hiding; it is about honoring your own value. It is about knowing that not everyone deserves a front-row seat to the details of your soul.

The Bible tells us in *Proverbs 17:27-28* that *"The one who has knowledge uses words with restraint, and whoever has understanding is even-tempered. Even fools are thought wise if they keep silent and discerning if they hold their tongues."*

Silence can be a form of wisdom, a divine pause that allows God to step in and speak on your behalf, to fight battles you cannot see, and to work in ways beyond your understanding.

Jesus understands this better than anyone. When He was falsely accused, He did not fight every word that was spoken against Him. *Isaiah 53:7* reminds us: *"He was oppressed and afflicted, yet He did not open His mouth; He was led like a lamb to the slaughter, and as a sheep before its shearers is silent, so He did not open His mouth."*

That is not weakness; it is divine strength. Jesus did not waste His breath trying to justify Himself to those who would not see the truth. He knew His mission, and He moved forward without being distracted by the noise of His critics or the weight of their misunderstanding.

This lesson resonates deeply with me as I think about the storms in my life. Growing up, weather storms were almost treated as sacred events by a few of my elders. When thunder shook the sky and lightning split the darkness, the house grew quiet. The lights were turned off. No one dared sit by the window. I remember seeing mirrors covered with sheets, a practice I never fully understood but instinctively respected. It was as though we were saying, we can't control this storm, but we can honor its power.

In many ways, life's storms deserve the same reverence. They may look destructive, but storms often reveal the strength of what remains. *Psalm 46:1-3* says, *"God is our refuge and strength, an ever-present help in trouble. Therefore, we will not fear, though the earth give way and the mountains fall into the heart of the sea, though its waters roar and foam and the mountains quake with their surging."*

Over time, I've learned not to fear the storm but to look for the lessons it carries. Storms have a way of shaking loose what wasn't supposed to stay, while also strengthening foundations built on faith.

For years, I tried to fit into molds that didn't reflect who I was. I wanted to be accepted. I wanted to be understood. But I have learned that true dignity comes when you stop forcing yourself into boxes that were never built for you. *Romans 12:2* reminds us, *"Do not conform to the pattern of this world, but be transformed by the renewing of your mind."*

Dignity and departure are about refusing to conform just to be accepted. It is about knowing when to walk away, leave the mold behind, and trust that God has something greater waiting beyond what you're leaving behind.

Shaking Off the Dust-Rising Higher

In the second part of this journey, I have come to embrace the power of walking away with grace and purpose. Departure is not simply about leaving something behind; it is about stepping into what is next with your head held high and your spirit aligned with God's will. *Ecclesiastes 3:1* tells us, *"There is a time for everything, and a season for every activity under the heavens."*

There is a time to speak and a time to be silent, a time to hold on and a time to let go. I think of the Morgan Freeman line from *The Shawshank Redemption*: *"Get busy living or get busy dying!"*

Jesus' life is filled with examples of dignified departure. He never lingered where He wasn't welcome. In *Matthew 10:14*, He told His disciples, *"If anyone will not welcome you or listen to your words, leave that home or town and shake the dust off your feet."*

That scripture resonates with me because there are times when I have clung too tightly to situations that no longer served me well. I've learned that it is not rejection when you walk away. It is redirection. It is God saying, *"There is something better ahead, something more aligned with your purpose and His plan."*

The storms of life are inevitable. We cannot predict them, and we cannot avoid them. But we can choose how we stand during them. Over the years, I have come to see storms as teachers. *James 1:2-4* encourages us, *"Consider it pure joy, my brothers and sisters, whenever you face trials of many kinds, because you know that the testing of your faith produces perseverance. Let perseverance finish its work so that you may be mature and complete, not lacking anything."*

Each storm I have endured has given me a new endurance, a deeper faith, and a clearer understanding of who I am in God.

This chapter of my life has taught me to let my actions and my silence speak louder than any explanation I could offer. I don't have to prove myself to anyone because God has already validated me. *Galatians 1:10* asks, *"Am I now trying to win the approval of human beings, or of God? Or am I trying to please people? If I were still trying to please people, I would not be a servant of Christ."*

These words remind me that my worth is rooted in Him, not in the opinions of others.

When I think about dignity in departure, it reminds me of the importance of trusting God's timing. Walking away is not about failure; it is about obedience. When God closes a door, it is because what's behind it is not intended for us, and He is preparing us to walk through a better door that He has already opened. It is about trusting that even when the storm rages, the same God who calmed the wind and waves with a single word (*Mark 4:39*) is still calming my storms today.

Guided Activity

Take 20 minutes of stillness today. Reflect on an area of your life where you need to walk away with dignity and respect. Write a letter expressing all the emotions and thoughts you would like to release. When you finish, pray over it and ask God to take those burdens. Tear up the letter as a symbol of letting go and moving forward.

Study Questions for Reflection

1. What does *Exodus 14:14* mean to you in seasons of transition?
2. How can silence be a form of strength in your life?
3. Reflect on a time when walking away preserved your dignity. What did you learn?
4. How do you see Jesus' example of graceful departure in your own life?
5. What storms have taught you resilience?
6. What molds or roles do you need to leave behind to be true to who God made you to be?
7. How do scriptures like *Romans 12:2* and *Galatians 1:10* encourage you to live authentically?
8. In what ways do you need to stop seeking validation from others?
9. How can you find peace in God's timing when leaving situations behind?

Closing Prayer

Lord, thank You for teaching me the power of dignity, silence, and letting go. Help me to walk away when You say it is time, to trust that You fight for me even when I am still. Give me the courage to let storms come, knowing they are shaping me into the person You have called me to be. May I stand firm, rooted in Your Word and Your love, as I step into the new seasons You have prepared for me. In Jesus' name, Amen.

CHAPTER ELEVEN
Commissioned Through the Cracks

Key Verse

"But we have this treasure in jars of clay to show that this all-surpassing power is from God and not from us." – 2 Corinthians 4:7

Opening Prayer

Heavenly Father, thank You for reminding me that my cracks are not my end, but the places where Your light shines through. Help me to see every broken part of my life as an opportunity for Your power to be revealed. Teach me that even when I feel weak, I am still called, chosen, and commissioned by You. Let my scars tell of Your goodness and Your grace. In Jesus' name, Amen.

Strength in the Silence of Fear

The day of my first scan to restage my tumor following my divorce remains etched in my mind as one of the most challenging yet defining moments of my journey. This wasn't just another medical appointment; it was an emotional battlefield where fear, faith, and the unknown collided. I reserved a room at a hotel adjacent to the hospital to avoid driving home after the scan since I had to return early the next morning for the results. I thought staying nearby would bring me convenience and peace of mind. But instead, it magnified the silence and the weight of my thoughts.

That night, my room was quiet except for my own sobs. Fear crept in with each passing hour, whispering "what if" into every corner of my mind. What if the cancer had grown? What if this was the beginning of something worse? What if I were truly alone in this battle? There is something about waiting for results that amplifies every insecurity, every scar from the past, and every moment of rejection. I lay in bed, clutching a pillow as if it could anchor me, and cried out to God, *"Lord, I don't know what to do. I don't know what tomorrow holds, but I need You to hold me through it."*

In that silence, my mind went back to another time when I walked these same halls, entered the same clinic, and was ushered into the same set of exam rooms awaiting the results of a scan. But at that time, it wasn't for me. It was for my mother. I recall being by her side when the doctor delivered the devastating news that her cancer had spread and there was nothing else they could do. I can still see her sitting there, holding back tears, and trying to be brave while she watched me shed tears that I tried desperately to hold back. I felt her pain deeply that day, but I also felt grateful that she didn't have to face it alone. In my hotel room, I thought about that moment and realized how much I longed for someone to stand with me now. But even if no one else was there, God was.

When morning came, I put on what I call my "game face." You learn to do that after years of battling not just illness, but also rejection, misunderstanding, and the challenges of life. I walked into the clinic, holding my head high while silently trembling on the inside. The waiting room was almost painfully quiet, and my thoughts screamed louder with every second that passed.

When my doctor walked in, his first question wasn't about my health. It was about my support system. *"Where's your husband? Where's your family?"* he asked.

That question, so simple yet so piercing, broke down the wall I had carefully built around my emotions. My eyes welled with tears as I quietly said, *"He's gone,"* explaining that we were now divorced. Then I added, almost defiantly, *"But I'm here."*

He looked at me with a mixture of compassion and firmness and said boldly, *"You take care of yourself. Let me worry about the cancer. That's what you pay me for."*

Those words were not just comforting; they were a divine message. In that moment, I felt the Lord whispering through the doctor's voice, *"My child, give it to Me. I've already carried this burden for you. You do not have to hold this alone."* Immediately, I thought of *1 Peter 5:7: "Cast all your anxiety on Him because He cares for you."*

I realized I had been holding onto fear as if it were my responsibility. But God doesn't ask us to carry fear. He calls us to release it. He reminds us that the battle belongs to Him (*2 Chronicles 20:15*). As I sat there, my tears turned from fear to gratitude. The doctor said the results were stable. The cancer hadn't grown, but it hadn't shrunk either. Some might see that as no progress, but I saw it as God holding the line. Stability is its own miracle.

This experience made me look at my cracks differently. Every tear, every sleepless night, every scar was not a weakness but places where God's light pours through. It is through these cracks that I have found a deeper faith, a renewed sense of purpose, and a greater understanding of His love. In my brokenness, I realized that I am still whole because He holds me.

Cracks That Commission

If the first part of this chapter is about the cracks that fear exposes, the second part is about the cracks God commissions. My story doesn't end with the doctor's words; it continues in the ways God uses my broken places to reach others. I think about a women's ministry in Dallas that invited me to speak. They had been reading my book, *God's*

Got it in the Bag, and as I stood before them, I could see the reflections of my journey in their faces. They were women who had faced rejection, illness, and heartache, yet they showed up hungry for hope.

Standing there, I understood something profound: my cracks were not disqualifiers. They were the very reasons I had something meaningful to share. I remembered *2 Corinthians 12:9*: *"But he said to me, 'My grace is sufficient for you, for my power is made perfect in weakness.' Therefore, I will boast all the more gladly about my weaknesses, so that Christ's power may rest on me."*

This verse isn't just scripture. It's a blueprint for living through the broken places.

At that particular time, I had been dealing for months with a horribly cracked and dangerously unsettled sidewalk leading up to the front door of my condo. I had been in a dispute with the homeowner's association because they refused to make the necessary repairs. At first, I was angry. I wanted it repaired so no one would trip, fall, and hurt themselves on the way into my house. One day, as I stood staring at that crack, God spoke to me. He reminded me that cracks are not always something to hide or fix. Sometimes, they're reminders of where we've been and what we've survived.

That sidewalk became a metaphor for my own life. I thought about all the emotional and spiritual cracks I carry, the places where life's storms had left marks on me. Just like that sidewalk, I realized I didn't need to be "perfectly paved" to keep walking. God uses every crack in my story as a pathway for someone else's healing. He turns brokenness into testimony each and every time. I felt this is what He was calling me to: expose my cracks, share my testimony, encourage, and lead another person to find their healing in God.

The Japanese art of Kintsugi beautifully illustrates this. In Kintsugi, broken pottery is repaired with gold, making the cracks the most valuable and beautiful part of the vessel. God's grace is the gold that fills our cracks. *Isaiah 61:3* reminds us that He gives us beauty for ashes, joy for mourning, and praise for despair. My life, with all its cracks, is proof that His light shines brightest through what I once saw as flaws.

As I shared my story with the Women's Group, I looked at the women in the room, and I could see their cracks, too. Some of them were fresh, while others had healed over time but were still visible. I hoped that they realized they were beautiful and that being cracked doesn't mean being useless. In fact, being cracked means you are more prepared to let God's light shine through.

We are all jars of clay (*2 Corinthians 4:7*), fragile but filled with treasure. The treasure is no less worthy because the jar is imperfect; if anything, the cracks allow the treasure to be seen. When I embraced that truth, I stopped hiding my scars. My battle with cancer, my experiences with rejection, my struggles with loneliness—they are all part of the gold-filled lines of my testimony.

Being commissioned through the cracks means accepting that God calls us not despite our brokenness, but because of it. Our stories of pain often become the very messages of hope that someone else desperately needs to hear. The cracks in our lives are not the end of our journey. They are evidence of grace, resilience, and redemption.

Guided Activity

On a blank piece of paper, draw a simple vessel or jar. Write down your "cracks" inside the jar: the challenges, fears, or moments of rejection that have shaped you. Around each crack, write how God has filled that space with grace, healing, or strength. Spend time in prayer, thanking Him for using your story, just as it is, to bring light to others.

Study Questions for Reflection

1. What cracks in your life have allowed God's power to shine through?
2. How do you relate to the message of *2 Corinthians 4:7*?
3. When have you seen God turn your fear into faith?
4. How does the Japanese art of Kintsugi speak to your journey of healing?
5. What testimony can you share that might bring hope to someone else?
6. How do you see beauty emerging from your scars?
7. How can you surrender your current battles to God and trust Him to fight for you?
8. How has your story inspired or encouraged someone else?
9. What does it mean to you to be commissioned through the cracks?
10. How can you celebrate God's work in your life this week?

Closing Prayer

Lord, thank You for the cracks that remind me of Your presence. Thank You for turning what I once saw as broken into something beautiful and filled with purpose. Teach me to see every scar as a testimony of Your power. Use my life to encourage others, and remind me that I am still called, still chosen, and still commissioned through every crack. In Jesus' name, Amen.

CHAPTER TWELVE
The Final Delivery—Signed, Sealed & Healed

Key Verse

"Therefore, go and make disciples of all nations, baptizing them in the name of the Father and of the Son and of the Holy Spirit, and teaching them to obey everything I have commanded you. And surely I am with you always to the very end of the age." – Matthew 28:19-20

Opening Prayer

Heavenly Father, thank You for bringing me to this moment — whole, healed, and held by You. As I prepare to close this chapter of pain and walk into a new chapter of purpose, help me to remember all You have delivered me from. Open my heart and mind to receive this final word of affirmation. Let it soak into my spirit as a reminder that my identity is in You, not in what I've been through. Let me walk boldly in freedom, with joy in my heart and purpose in my step. In Jesus' name, Amen.

Walking Out of the Post Office of Pain

There is a deep, sacred power in the imagery of walking out of the "post office of pain"—hands empty, heart light, and spirit free. For years, I carried letters of disappointment and envelopes of unspoken hurt, tucked away like undelivered messages in my soul. Rejection after rejection piled up like unopened mail, marked "Return to Sender" as though my worth and love were never enough for those who once claimed to care for me. But now, I see with clarity that every missed delivery was not the end. It was a reroute, a divine redirection toward the path God always intended for me.

Life has its way of testing our resolve. I remember vividly the frustration of living in an apartment complex where mailboxes and mail were constantly mixed up. Vital letters, bank statements, and important notices ended up in the wrong hands or were discarded altogether. I cannot count how many times I walked to my box only to find someone else's mail staring back at me, a reminder that what was intended for me had been misplaced. It became so discouraging that I finally made a choice. I went to the post office and rented a post office box so I could have a secure place to receive what belonged to me.

That decision taught me something more profound about life and faith. We often hand our hearts and dreams to people who are ill-equipped to handle them. We trust individuals—friends, partners, colleagues—with our most delicate feelings, only to see them tossed aside, forgotten, or misinterpreted. But just as I found security and order with a P.O. box, I have found divine order by entrusting my heart to God. He is the Master Sorter. He never loses track of a single prayer, a single tear, or a single desire. His timing is perfect, and His delivery is always right on time.

As I reflect on this final delivery, I am reminded of my wedding day. Stevie Wonder's *"Signed, Sealed, Delivered, I'm Yours"* played as we exited the ceremony. A declaration that we were all in, united, and committed. Back then, those lyrics were a promise of love. But life has a way of shifting and testing even the most substantial commitments. What we thought would last forever unraveled, and I found myself standing in the ruins of promises, unsure of how to move things forward but determined to find healing.

Yet here is what I've come to understand: though relationships can change, God's love remains steadfast. My life is now signed with His name, sealed by His Spirit, healed by His grace, and delivered back into His hands. I am not broken mail or discarded love. I am a divine message of hope and resilience, written by the Creator Himself and sent into this world for a purpose. That realization is my holy exhale. The deep breath of surrender when you know you no longer have to chase what's meant for you because what God has ordained for you will always find its way into your life at the right time, without you having to force it.

This first part of my journey is about release. It's about walking out of that "post office of pain" with empty hands but a whole heart, knowing that everything I once mourned has been placed into the capable hands of God. *Romans 12:2* calls us to be *"transformed by the renewing of your mind,"* and this renewal has been my greatest gift. I am no longer stamped with the labels of rejection or failure. I am His masterpiece, His beloved daughter. Signed, sealed, healed, and delivered!

Misdelivered Mail and the Great Commission

Misdelivered mail holds a special place in my memory because of the lessons it has taught me about destiny and divine timing. I used to believe that when something was misplaced—an opportunity, a relationship, or a dream—it was lost forever. But now I know better. God is in the business of divine redirection. Just as I once had to claim my misdelivered letters from the post office, God has claimed every misplaced hope and redirected it toward my purpose.

One of the most powerful revelations I have had is that healing is not about returning to who I used to be, but about becoming who God always intended me to be.

The memory of Stevie Wonder's song has taken on new meaning for me. "Signed, Sealed, Delivered, I'm Yours" is no longer a song about earthly commitment; it is my declaration to God. I am all in. I am His, with no reservations and no conditions. My life is a love letter to my Creator, and with every chapter of pain and healing is a line of testimony written in grace.

This final chapter is about your dedication to rising. It is about acknowledging that even though we have been bent, folded, and marked by life's journeys, we are still a "letter" worth delivering.

And now, we are delivered to God. There is no safer, more loving destination. Rejection is no longer my identity. Grace is. Faith is. Purpose is. My story is a reflection of *Philippians 1:6*—He who began a good work in me is faithful to complete it. I am walking forward, not just as someone who survived, but as someone who thrives under the care of the One who never loses track of His creation.

As you complete this reading, I pray you feel the strength of every lesson and story woven into its pages. This isn't just my journey; it's an invitation for you to rise from your own "post office of pain," to see every rejection as redirection, and every crack as a canvas for God's grace. You are not lost or forgotten. You are signed by His love, sealed by His promises, healed by His mercy, and delivered into a purpose greater than you can imagine. Go forward with hope, knowing that your story—just as it is—has the power to inspire and transform the world around you.

Guided Activity

Take time today to write your own "final delivery letter." Start with, "Dear Me, I am signed, sealed, healed, and delivered..." Pour out every truth you have discovered through your journey. Seal the letter in an envelope, and on the outside, write: "Return to Sender: God's Masterpiece." Keep this letter in a safe place as a reminder of who you are and how far you have come.

Study Questions for Reflection

1. How does the image of "misdelivered mail" resonate with your personal experiences?
2. What does it mean for you to walk out of your own "post office of pain?"
3. How does *Philippians 1:6* encourage you in your current season of life?
4. How has God used rejection to redirect you toward your true purpose?
5. What steps can you take to embrace being fully "signed, sealed, healed, and delivered?"
6. How can you apply the Great Commission to share your testimony of healing with others?
7. What song, scripture, or memory reminds you of your commitment to God?
8. What message of hope can you deliver to someone who feels forgotten or lost?
9. How do you see God's faithfulness reflected in the chapters of your life?
10. What does your "holy exhale" look like as you enter a new season of purpose?

Closing Prayer

Lord, thank you for carrying me through every misstep and missed opportunity in my life. I am signed by Your love, sealed with Your Spirit, healed by Your mercy, and delivered to Your purpose. As I close this chapter, I open my heart to the future You have planned for me. May my life be a letter of hope, encouragement, and unwavering faith. In Jesus' name. Amen.

ACKNOWLEDGMENTS

To my dear friend and Sister, Angie Ransome-Jones, I thank you for your belief in my writing once again and your dedication to ensuring my story is told.

To Genice Johnson, my amazing editor and friend, I thank you for consistently reviewing my work to ensure its perfection and the smooth flow of my words and thoughts. You are the cherry on the top.

To Maurice Rogers, my wonderfully talented cover artist, I thank you once again for bringing my vision of a soothing, nightstand-worthy book cover to life, one that evokes a sense of peace.

To my awesome typesetter, Keith Kareem Williams, I extend my gratitude for ensuring that the pages of this book are visually appealing and laid out in a manner that promotes ease of reading and smooth transition.

To my beautiful Beta Readers, I thank you for your candid feedback, testimonials, and dedication of time to ensure my message was truly conveyed to readers.

www.ingramcontent.com/pod-product-compliance
Lightning Source LLC
Chambersburg PA
CBHW050652160426
43194CB00010B/1904